The
Alabama
Ironman

Jody & Steph

Ya'll were great to
work with, glad I could
help! Go N' Bless your
family, Don't ever
give up —

Joh
mt

7-7-07

Matthew 7:7,8
Hebrews 12:1

The
Alabama
Ironman

The Authorized Biography of
Johnny Montgomery

by Jerry W. Henry

LEGACY PUBLISHING SERVICES

602 N. Wymore Road Winter Park, Florida 32789

www.LegacyPublishingServices.com

Photograph of the statue "Man Carving His Own Destiny" by Albin Polasek, is used with the permission of the Albin Polasek Museum and Sculpture Gardens, 633 Osceola Avenue, Winter Park, Florida 32790. Visit their website at *www.polasek.org* or call 407-647-6294.

Published by:
LEGACY PUBLISHING SERVICES, INC.
602 N. Wymore Road
Winter Park, Florida 32789
www.legacypublishingservices.com

Copyright © 2005 by Jerry W. Henry
3rd printing August 2005
ISBN   0-9708395-0-2
Cover Design by Gabriel H. Vaughn

For comments to the author, scheduling interviews or speaking engagements, contact through the *authors'* page at www.legacypublishingservices.com.

Printed in United States of America

Foreword

The odds against Johnny Montgomery and I ever writing a book using the English language must be phenomenal. I went to school with Johnny, starting at the Junior High level. Throughout high school we were both D and F students. With this background, I hope you readily understand why I don't call myself an author, but instead call myself a biographical interviewer.

It's quite a contrast to see Johnny in his surroundings now; remembering his past from those days at Montgomery's Store. Johnny has greatly changed for the better. This book is about his life and these changes. God works in mysterious ways, and I think this book proves it.

Special thanks to: God, Johnny Montgomery, the people that were interviewed, Bobby S.(manuscript editor), and Patricia E. (typist). I also want to thank Deana Freeland for her patience and understanding. Deana is a musician, and was releasing her first international single, a beautiful song entitled "Mother Teresa," at the same time I was writing this book. I just want to say, "Thanks, Deana," for bearing with me, your producer, during those times when there wasn't enough time.

Table of Contents

Johnny Montgomery
First Interview

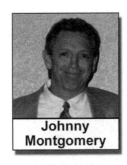

Johnny
Montgomery

JWH - Johnny, as far back as I can remember you've been setting records. Does any of those high school or college records still stand?

Johnny - I don't know if my high school or college records still stand because it's something I don't keep up with. I don't know if they still keep records over at Tuscaloosa County High School in Northport, (AL) or not. I do remember coach Eubanks used to keep them on the wall over there. I used to be on the wall with some real fast times in the state in the 180 low hurdles, the 120 yard high hurdles, and the broad jump. I used to have a bunch of them over there. At Livingston University, (Livingston, AL) I held the high hurdle record, low board hurdles, broad jump, and again I still don't know if they're still there or not. Athletes have gotten bigger, faster, and stronger since I left from there. If anything, I think the high hurdle would be hard to beat. All that's something I never kept up with.

JWH - Going back to high school, coach Eubanks must have been an influence on you?

Johnny - We called him Bulldog, and you're right. He had a great influence on me. He's the one that got me into competitive running. Before that all my running had been on the farm chasing cows. I knew I could run a long time, because it took a long time to chase those cows into the barn. I've been running all my life. I can remember back in Taylorville Elementary when Bill Bradley was the fastest guy in school. I knew when I out ran him I had something.

Coach Eubanks got me running track because I could do it during school hours. All the other sports like baseball, football, or basketball were practiced after school. I had to be on that school bus to get home by 3:30 to milk cows and shovel cow manure. There was always something that had to be done.

I was either working around the store or working in the fields on the farm. I always wanted to play the other sports, and it really hurt me that I didn't get to. I know I could have played with them boys if I could have had the chance.

Coach Eubanks was my first mentor. He could see I had some talent and he was willing to work with me. He was a good disciplinarian, too. He would ride me pretty hard when he knew I was messing up.

I remember when coach Williams was coaching football in our senior year. He talked me into coming out to play foot-

High School Race - 1963

ball. I think at the time Butch Lary was about the only receiver we had, but I was the fastest guy on the track team and coach Williams was aware of me. Curley Hallman was quarterback. He was really good, but he didn't have anybody to throw to, so I came out and practiced all week long, and knew I was going to be a football star for sure. I remember we played Northside High School, and coach Williams kept saying, "Yea, Johnny, we're going to put you in any minute." I was ready. I had mama and daddy sitting up in the stands, and I was ready. Well, back then the kids used to throw Dixie cups full of our Alabama red clay at each other. One of these Dixie cups lands on the sidelines and happens to hit me on the shoulder of my uniform. So I took this clay and rub it all over my uniform. It made it seem like I'd seen a lot of action, but really I hadn't left the bench. Then the game is over and I come jogging off the field and run into one of the benches. I knocked a big knot on my leg and I come limping into the field house with my pride hurt from not being allowed in the game. Coach Williams laughed and asked if I'd been clipped, knowing he never even let me in the game. I was very upset that night. I took a shower and got dressed, and when I went out the field house door there was Coach Eubanks waiting for me. He pulled me over to the side, looked me in the eye and said, "Montgomery, you're never going to get a scholarship playing football, but you can get a scholarship running." He told me you either be on that track Monday morning or you'll never run at this school again. Needless to say, I was out running on that track bright and early next Monday morning. That was the end of my football career. Yep, coach Eubanks kept me focused after that.

JWH - I remember you playing baseball on a black team. What was that all about?
Johnny - During the summer I played semi-pro baseball with the Jerusalem Cubs. They had a field over behind Dreamland Barbecue. I played semi-pro baseball for them for nine years. We had some outstanding teams during those years. I played center field, I hit a lot of home runs, and I never got thrown out stealing bases during those nine years. We traveled all over the South, played against Charles Cleveland, the great ball player from Bibb County. I really enjoyed playing with those guys. I always wanted to play baseball and that gave me the chance. It also gave me a chance to drink cold beer. They kept coolers under the pine trees for us to drink. Pop Russell ran things and he seemed good at it. There would be hundreds of folks that would come out and watch us play. If you made a homer they would pass the hat for you. Sometimes you could make 30 or 40 dollars for a homerun. That was good money in those days. Pop charged a buck to get into the game, and that was how he paid us, a few bucks at a time, plus all the beer and barbecue we could eat and drink. A band would start playing about the seventh inning. That same band played at his nightclub over by the right field fence. Live music always draws folks and Pop would charge another dollar to get into his club. Ol' Pop had it wired, he had two gates working. He was a entrepreneur.

JWH - You were playing interracial baseball here in the deep South during the civil rights movement. How did that feel?

Johnny - I didn't think anything about it. Back then, my daddy had 25 to 50 blacks working for him on the farm at a time. During hay bailing or cotton picking time he sometimes had more. We all worked together on the farm. In the mornings when we went out to work, I jumped on the truck like everybody else. There were blacks and whites doing a days work. There is no racial strife in a setting like that. When they brought the water in milk jugs later that day everybody drank from the same jugs. There was none of this is my water fountain, and that is your water fountain stuff out there. The only thing I didn't care for was when J.B. Harper would be eating chicken and some of it would backwash into the water jug. I really didn't care for that, but you would be so thirsty you would close your eyes and take a drink anyway.

When we would come in from the fields in the afternoon daddy would have a couple of cases of beer, and as we were waiting for our pay he would throw these beers out into the yard like you would feeding the chickens corn. We would all get out there and fight for those beers like chickens would for corn.

JWH - What happened after high school?

Johnny - When I graduated Tuscaloosa County High School in 1964 I signed with the University of Alabama. Of course I was too dumb to get in. I was a Proposition 48. Most people didn't know what that was back then . That's all you read about in the newspaper now a days. That means you go off to a Junior College your first two years. I couldn't get into Alabama, so I said, heck, I don't need to go to school anyway. I'm going to pump gas, shovel cow manure, and bootleg the rest of my life. That's what my mama and daddy did and they done all right. So I laid out a year. In the meantime my brother got me and Mickey Nix to join the National Guard because he got a $5 bonus for every person he got to sign up. I joined because I wanted some boots. Looking back, that seems like a hell of a thing to do, join the National Guard for six years just to get a pair of free boots.

Red Drew had been the coach at Alabama, but then Billy Hardin came in. Billy was still going to give me a scholarship to go to Alabama. I took all of these GED tests because I made several F's in English in high school. I had to average 50 by the time I finished taking all these test, and I think that I got a 49.6. I will never forget that for the rest of my life. I won't mention his name, but the Dean said, "Mister Montgomery, according to all these tests you aren't going to be very successful." I'll tell you what, that statement is still burned into my brain. I don't know what he considered success. If it's material things, then just look around, what more could I want?

I had to go to Livingston University, in Livingston, Alabama. I got a scholarship to go down there. I was going to go there for a year and then transfer back up to Alabama for three more years. At least that was the plan at the time.

In high school I could do all the track and field events. Livingston, being a small school, gave me a chance to do the same thing; compete in all the events. Sometimes I would compete in eight or 10 events just to score a lot of points. But I'd

Miss Livingston University Kissing Freshman Cake Race Winner

specialize in the 440 hurdles, broad jump, triple jump, and the high hurdles to get to the next level. If I'd went to Alabama I'd have run in only 2 or 3 events.

JWH - What were your best events?

Johnny - It was the probably the 440 hurdles, the high hurdles, or the steeplechase. With the speed and coordination I'd got running hurdles it had to be. But Jerry, I never got to specialize, so we'll never know what I might have really excelled at if I'd specialized in just one or two events.

JWH - Did you ever make it to Alabama?

Johnny - My first year down there in Livingston I got an F in English, so I never had the grades to transfer to Alabama. But I look back on it now and it was a lesson in disguise, because my brother owned three beer joints on the strip in Tuscaloosa, and I probably would have lived in them.

Sumter county was dry when I first went to Livingston in 1966. While I was there it became one of my goals to make Sumter county wet. I didn't like traveling so far to get my cold beer. Before I graduated from Livingston, Sumter county was wet.

If I had gone to Alabama I know for a fact I would never have graduated. I got a B.S. degree from Livingston. I tell everybody that stands for bowling and shuffleboard. I literally worked my way through college on bowling matches, shuffleboard, and shootin' pool. That's the way I made my money. If you walked into a beer joint then I was going to get your money. Plus I was going to get all the cold beer that I, and everybody with me could drink. I would actually go into some of these places with literally only a quarter in my pocket. Just enough to play one of these machines. Just enough to get me a bet for a quarter. Then a couple of hours later I would leave there with a couple of hundred dollars and two sacks of beer, and had a good time, too. That was just part of surviving. It was like bootlegging on the farm. It wasn't to make money. It was to keep the banker from taking our farm. Hustling in these beer joints was for survival. It was a means to get gas money; and money to eat on.

JWH - Did this ever result in violence? Where there's a pool table in a bar, there's a fight in the making. Ever heard that?

Johnny - Oh yea, where there's alcohol there's fights. Period. I always avoided that stuff. I was the peacemaker and a good negotiator. Maybe that's why I'm in sales now.

There was a lot of violence in my background. Us, being bootleggers, gave me lots of chances to see shootins', cuttins', and killin's. There was a lot of violence back then. Where there's alcohol there's always going to be violence. I've seen daddy beat people with Coke bottles. I've seen him cut people with his knife. I saw daddy get cut by his own brother-in-law. Mother shot at me with a pistol once because I took her alcohol away from her. I've been beaten by my sisters ex-husband. He put a shotgun to my head once. I've seen a lot of violence. When people get excited it scares me. I was told, Johnny you may have a lot of rage inside you,. But I feel I've worked through a lot of that stuff.

The prisons are full of people as a result of violence. In one of those prisons is the guy that murdered my mother. This guy had murdered someone else in 1954, and was on death row. He got out, and within two months he had murdered my mother. I believe that if they had put that man in the electric chair, the way it was supposed to have been, then my mother might still be alive today. I believe in capital punishment. But instead he's over here in prison and I've been debating whether to go over and forgive this guy or not. I'm seriously considering doing this.

JWH - Johnny, do you mind explaining what happened to your mother?

Johnny - I was the last one to leave home, and as you know we operated Montgomery's Store on U.S. Highway 82. That's the Montgomery highway just south of Tuscaloosa. The store was a two story structure with a fire engine sitting out front. That store was a landmark in that area for sure.

Well, my mama took in strays. She took in good ones like Jim Johnson. This guy flies us to every Superbowl. He'll call up and say, "Are you Montgomery boys ready to go?" He's a multi-millionaire, but back then it was mama who fed him and kept him alive. He went on to own one of the largest car dealerships in the country. He gives us free tickets to the Superbowl and flies us there, no matter where it's being played. He's flown us to Canada to fish and hunt. He does all this because mama took him in way back when.

But once mama got a few drinks in her, you didn't mess

with her liquor, her money, or her stuff. Material things meant a lot back then.

Once I left Tuscaloosa it left mama to run the store. Times were changing. Instead of just alcohol there were drugs to contend with. Drug people would just walk in, rob you, and blow you away because they didn't want you to identify them.

Mama got involved with this guy who was just out of prison. He was supposedly there to help her and protect her while she was running the store. But this guy was an alcoholic too, and once he had a few drinks he got violent. What happened that night I don't know. But I will tell you how smart the guy was. He and mama were drinking that night and they got into a fight. I think he took some of mama's money, or something. Anyway, he shot mama 3 times. He shot her once in the jaw, once in the shoulder, and then when she was down, he shot her in the head. He put that gun to her head and shot her that third time to make sure she was dead. He then took time to drink up all the liquor that was left and stuff all of mama's money into his pockets, and then he picked up the phone and called the Tuscaloosa Police Department to tell them they had better get over there, because Miss Montgomery had committed suicide. This tells us the brilliance of the guy . After they arrest him he's sitting in the back seat of the patrol car pulling money out of his pockets saying, "I'm somebody now, I've got money." That's what the Police said, anyway.

That was another low point in our lives. Daddy had cancer, but that came from smoking and drinking, and was long and drawn out. But when someone is murdered, and they are taken from you so fast, that's hard to digest.

JWH - How old were you when all this happened?

Johnny - Mother got murdered in 1977, and daddy died in 1976. Right there in about a year's span we had a tough time. Daddy died, mother got murdered, and my wife was kidnapped; all within a year.

The same day we buried mother was the same day we found out my wife, Susan, was pregnant with my daughter Meredith. It was like God took someone away, but at the same time gave us someone back.

Through all these trials and tribulations there was always some liquid medicine that I could drink down to medicated myself against all these problems. I could medicate myself and not feel the real pain. Alcohol was my crutch to get me through these times.

JWH - You said your wife was kidnapped. Tell us about that.

Johnny - That was a very tough year. In that year, daddy died, mama got murdered, and my wife's father died. It was like, what else can happen. Susie worked for Pizitz department store. The day she was kidnapped she was leaving early from work to get ready for a wedding. Usually, all of the women left together. But on this day she left early in order to beat traffic. She got on the elevator with two men. When the elevator stopped, she walked to her car in the parking deck. But when she got to her car they were right on top of her. They pulled knives on her and made her get into her car. She had a Pinto back then, the kind with the two bucket seats up front. They made her sit on the console between the two seats, but had problems cranking the car because the seat belts had to be fastened before the car would start, and they didn't know that. They finally did get it started though, and drove out of the lot right by the security booth. The lady in the security booth had been working there for years, and here was Susie sitting between two bad looking dudes in her own car, and the lady never even looked up. Here was a scene that was totally out of the ordinary, and lady never even noticed! She said by this time she was in shock. One of them held a knife to her side and told her not to scream or try anything. They started talking about all the bad things they would do to her. At the point when they were leaving town she started realizing they were going to kill her. She was thinking, "I'm going to be dead."

When they got out to Fultondale they got stuck in traffic. At that moment, Susie prayed, "Please dear God get me out of this!" and she slid back between the seats. She got her hand up to the door handle on the driver's side, opened the door, and pushed herself out between the seat and the car frame. She got out through that door opening onto the pavement, and everyone trapped in that traffic saw what happened. The guys got away by driving on the shoulder of the road and escaping through all that traffic. Some people got out of their cars and went with Susie into a hotel and called the police. A couple of days later they found her car in Coalburg. They strip cars there, and they had tried to run her car into a strip pit. A little tree caught the car, so it never went out of sight like they had intended. About a month later, they caught those guys. One of them was loose and on the streets, but the other one had been convicted of armed robbery, and had been out on parole when they kidnapped Suzie. It seems like sometimes the bad just get badder. Suzie is very lucky to be alive. The Lord was with her that day, but it changed her a lot. She became scared all the time. I would go to take the garbage out and she would deadbolt the door after me. Even today, she is extremely scared and over-protective.

JWH - When I'm around you I get flashbacks of high school. What do you remember most about high school?

Johnny - Remember Pauline Neighbors? I remember the day we were supposed to graduate from Tuscaloosa County High School. Now, as you know I always liked to have a lot of fun. I wasn't the class clown, but I did sit next to him, so I learned a lot of fun stuff. But I never will forget the day Miss Pauline Neighbors the day were to get our cap and gown. She came in and said, "Johnny, you and Mickey Nix aren't going to graduate because you two flunked English again this semester." I said, "Miss Pauline, it's going to be a pleasure spending another year with you." She took off and went straight to the principles office, George Hataway. She was gone about and hour and a half and then she came back into the room and said, "Johnny, you and Mickey go and get your caps and gowns. Ya'll are going to graduate tonight." She knew if she had me and Mickey one more year it would have driven her straight into the Bryce mental facility.

JWH - Did you get married right out of college?

Johnny - We dated 5 years. We took it slow and made sure that's what we wanted to do, so we dated 5 years, and we were married 16-that's 21 years. I think I got married when I was 26. Her name was Susie Luxich and we had a lot in common. Her dad was a flaming alcoholic, and so was her mom. But Susie was not an alcoholic.

I handle divorces everyday in my business. I live with all the problems that divorce creates. Me and Susie don't have those problems. We get along better than any other divorced couple I know. I went over there to pick Megan up. Her husband, Rod, came to the door and I told him I wished him a happy Fathers Day, or rather, a happy step-Fathers Day. I told him that sometimes he treats my kids better than I do. I told him how much I really did want him to know I appreciated him. All three of us have a great relationship.

JWH - Was alcohol the reason for your divorce?

Johnny - Yes it was. You can point a finger and say this thing happened, or that thing happened, but the bottom line reason was alcohol. I don't know if I'd quit beer before our divorce-I don't know if it would have saved our marriage or not.

JWH - How old were you when you drank your first beer?

Johnny - Daddy told me he first started giving me beers when I was 5 years old. We would be on our way to Swain's stockyard, going to the cow sales. Of course daddy would have him a pint up under the seat, and a six pack up on the seat between us. He would let me drink one or two and get me to sing. He didn't have a radio in his truck.

To help pay the bills my folks did some bootlegging. Clyde Bolton did an article on me a few years ago and I told him some of my fastest times ever was running through the woods without a clock on me, because I knew if I got caught I would wind up down in Kilby prison making car tags.

JWH - Johnny, as great an athlete as you have been, have you ever considered how great you might have been without the drinking?

Johnny - I guess the reason I like to compete on a world level now-like, I just got back from Switzerland competing with best in the world-and I've been in the Ironman in Hawaii seven times already, and hopefully I'll be go going back for the 8th time this year, is that I always try to be the best. Even in high school I wanted to be state champion. Back then I had dreams and goals of running in the Olympics. I had seen the Jim Thorpe story, and he was just a poor Indian farmer. I could relate to that because I was just a poor dirt farmer. We didn't have running water. We didn't get plumbing in the house until I was in the 10th grade. We got a black and white TV that year, too. But before that I was the pot man. I'm the one that took the pots out and cleaned them. I also carried the well water to the house. Sure I'm only 54, but there's a lot of folks that can relate to that this day and time. But still our mama's and daddy's had it worse than we did. And now we got kids whining because we only have 2 VCR's and 7 TV sets.

I had dreams of going to the Olympics, but that can of beer was a lot more important back then.

JWH- We know you hustled your way through college. Did the drinking continue after college?

Johnny - All I went to college for was to run and drink. But then something happened that was a turning point in my life. One day I was sitting around the store reading the newspaper when I overheard my mama telling someone that Johnny was the only one who ever went to college and he's going to graduate next year. "I'm going to be so proud of him," I heard her say. And I said to myself, "Oh my God, if she only knew how bad my grades really were." At the time I was about as far from graduating as they were from putting a man on the moon. Of course in 1970 they did put a man on the moon, and I did graduate. Unknown to my mama she gave me the inspiration to put out the effort to graduate. It's amazing what you can do when you know you got to do something. That's the way us alcoholic people are, we don't do anything until we have to do it. 'Till this day I still work better under pressure.

It's like last night, I had a Blues Brothers gig to do. I had all week long to get everything together. I had to be at the gig at 6 o'clock. At 5:30 I'm over here putting everything in the bag and fighting the clock to get there on time.

Back to your question, my drinking actually increased when I got out of college. When I got out of college I didn't have a job. I was going back to shoveling manure, picking cotton, and bootlegging whiskey. That's all I knew how to do. I was running the store with mama, and she was a flaming alcoholic. We kept all that beer there, and all I had to do was reach across the counter and get one any time I wanted it.

We got robbed one night. I remember it was when Monday night football started coming on television. Me and mama was having us a few cold ones while watching the game. The first thing I know some guy comes through the door and puts a shotgun up to my head. He robs us of a couple of hundred dollars. He puts us in the back of the store and tells us, "If you come out of that back room I'm going to blow both of your heads off." Me and Mama had enough liquid courage in us that once he drove off we got out our pistols to start chasing him. We jumped in our car but couldn't get the thing to crank. That's when we figured out the thing was out of gas. We had to put gas in that car before we could take off in hot pursuit. Of course I had called the police before the chase started. The police caught him when he had to stop at a train down at the AGS Depot. That guy could have blown our brains out if we had been the one's that caught him. Later on, when things had settled down, we realized just how stupid we were to chase that guy. If we hadn't been drinking we would have never considered anything like that. We lost a hundred dollars on the Green Bay Packers that same night. It was an upsetting night. But it gave me and mama the excuse to go to one of Jimmy's bar's and spend the rest of the night. Jimmy is my brother.

JWH - Which bar's did Jimmy own?

Johnny - The Wooden Door, The Brass Monkey, and several more along the way. It was a haven for free beer for me.

JWH - Let's talk about Jimmy now.

Johnny - Jimmy should be dead by now too, because of the car wrecks, fights, and driving to and from football games when he was falling down drunk. It's amazing he's still alive today, but now he's the epitome of fatherhood. He's got a daughter he truly loves. He's got a wife that stood beside him in all his drunken times. Why she stayed, I don't know. I used to beg her to leave him. He's really into his family now. He says if his daughter comes in and says, "Dad, I'm bored, lets do something." Jimmy says, "You can bet your butt, we're going to find something to do." And it's the same with my girls. When they say, "Hey dad, lets do something." Then we go jump on our bikes and go down to the Shell station and get a snack, or to the Anchorage and eat breakfast, or the park; or just go anywhere and do something. There's a whole lot of difference between where we were then and where we are now.

During the last 2 or 3 years of his drinking I wouldn't go around him at all. I kept my kids away from him, too. I was straight and I didn't want to hear that same old crap coming from him that I had heard all those years. Once you get sober, you don't want to hear all that crap.

When we went to Hawaii last year that was the first time he had ever been there sober. I've been to Hawaii seven times, and five of those time he was laid up in bed drunk. But the last time he actually got to see the race. He got to see what was going on. He got to see what it's all about. Normally, in Hawaii, he and Jeanette would go to the grocery store and get a cart and fill it with beer, Crown Royale, vienna sausages, potted meat, sardines, pork-and-beans, crackers, and tabasco sauce. They would then roll that cart over into their hotel room and live out of it for a week. That's just the way they liked to live. But now they want to eat in nice restaurants. They're healthy and they sure seem to enjoy themselves.

JWH - How much of an influence was Jimmy on your life?

Johnny - He was my daddy. I didn't know it at the time, but he was my role model. That's why once I gave up drinking there was a lot of anger. He was my role model. He couldn't help it, he didn't want to be my role model, but he was. He was my daddy. He's the one that gave me money, cars, whatever I needed. He taught me how to drive, drink, raise hell, and cut up. He taught me a lot of bad things because I watched him, and that's what he was doing. I just followed along in his foot-steps. I copied Jimmy. I wasn't a separate person in my own right, I was just a spin off of Jimmy. Everybody used to kid me and say you act just like Jimmy. You and Jimmy are just alike. As long as I was still drinking that sounded good because I really thought he was somebody. And he is somebody, he's quite a character. You might should be writing a story about him.

But once I got sober I'd listen to everything he said. And a lot of things I thought was true, I realized that they were alco-holic words coming from the mouth of an alcoholic mind. Now I know that's the part you've got to change. And you have it all the time. Well, he's not ever going to change, but I can change if I want to. The difference between a rut and a grave is the grave's just a little bit deeper.

We worked hard all our lives and Mama and Daddy treated us pretty rough. Not that that gave us an excuse to go out and do the things we did because we all have a choice. You can either do right or you can do wrong. When you hear about some-body from the wrong side of the tracks getting into trouble, you hear that he didn't have a proper upbringing, or he didn't have enough education. That's a bunch of crap. That guy, whether he's got a first grade education, or a doctors degree, has a choice. It's a choice of if I'm going to do right, or I'm going to do wrong. Either way it's a choice.

Jimmy gave me some real bad habits. I liked them, but I knew I couldn't keep up with him. I saw that way of life was going to be my life, as it was my daddy's life, my mama's life, and my granddaddy's life. I knew there had to more to life. And there is.

There's a whole lot more to life for me now. Things mean a whole lot more. Even material things like houses, cars, boats, clothes. All those things. Yea, I've got all that and they mean a lot more now because I'm willing to share them. I look on these things in a different light.

Johnny - Jimmy quit drinking 5 years ago. When I quit drinking I realized that this chemical dependency that ran through us was killing all of us. It had killed my daddy and mother. She got murdered down there in that store, but it was because of alcohol. It was killing me. It was killing my brother, and when I went through a divorce, I remembered I never had a daddy that was there for me. I never had a mother that was there for me. 'Till this day I never knew my mama or daddy. I don't remember them hugging me or telling me I love you, or even them saying Johnny, you're doing a good job.

That's why when I talk to the girls today, even on the phone, I tell them; I love you, I care about you, you're doing a great job. They need that, and I know that's what I always wanted.

JWH - Can you remember your turning point?

Johnny - After my divorce I was sitting around the house one day. My two girls were there. They were 2 and 12 years old, and they were watching TV. Their ol' dad was laid up on the couch with them, Miller High Life's beer cans stacked up by the my side of the couch. Back then we called them Bobby Allison's, because Bobby was driving a race car for Miller beer. Anyway, I'm laying there with them Bobby Allison cans scattered around and, Jerry, it was like somebody took a TV camera and panned back up to the ceiling of that room, and I can see this ol' drunk daddy laying there with his two beautiful daughters watching TV. They were hungry, needin' a daddy, needin' feedin'-and I said to myself-I don't like this picture. . .I don't like this picture at all. I've seen this before. I was raised up this way, and from that day on I haven't touched a can of beer. That was 10 years ago.

JWH - Why that day?

Johnny - Even though I was drinking, it was like I knew this ain't going to work. It ain't working for nobody. Then on top of that we were bootleggers. As bootleggers that's all we saw stum-

Megan, Johnny and Meredith Montgomery

bling in the door. There to pawn their work tools, their pistols, their diamond rings, watches, spare tires, guitars. Anything to get that alcohol.

JWH - What was the worst you saw?

Johnny - The worst I ever saw was this guy that used to walk all the way from Cottondale to my daddy's house. He would leave his cowboy boots for a pint of wildcat whiskey and walk all the way back to Cottondale barefoot. Now think about it. Who's in control here? When you walk five miles up a dirt road, leave your boots, and walk all the way back in your sockfeet. Now that's a problem.

If you got the disease, then until you stop drinking, you're in denial. And as you know , denial is not a river in Egypt. Denial is whenever you don't want to face reality. Denial is the shock absorber of the body. Denial will work for you until you can adjust, face, and handle reality. But you have to face reality sooner or later. You can't live in denial all your life.

Once I quit drinking I could see all these things. I could look at the history of the whole Montgomery family. Alcohol killed my granddaddy. It's like a fire going through a sage field. It's killing everyone of us. And I knew if I didn't do something about it, who would? Am I going to let alcohol run my girls lives?

I admitted that, yes, my girls might have the disease. The least I can do is be an example for them. I didn't have a role model. I didn't have a daddy who was there, and then I had this brother that was a flaming alcoholic. I look back now, and I see I carried a lot of anger once I got sober because here's this guy that's my role model, but what kind of role model was he?

I started praying for my brother once I quit drinking. I knew he had to get sober before he killed himself. He loved Crown Royale. Here's this guy that's my role model, but what kind of role model was he? I never thought he would quit drinking because he loved it too much. He loved Crown Royale more than fish love water.

The last time I saw Jimmy drinking, he had been out on one of those 4 or 5 day benders. As usual, his wife was calling me, upset and all. I told her, Ruth, leave him. Pack up and come over here. I told her alcohol was more important to Jimmy than anything. More important than her, his family, food; anything. You name it. When he came in, he had fell down somewhere and broke his nose. I knew it wouldn't be long before he would be dead. I just knew it. I got in my car and drove all the way to Tuscaloosa and went to his house. He was laying there on the couch, blood-shot eyes, looking like you usually look after you had been drinking for 4 or 5 days. I looked him dead in the eye and said, "I drove all the way down here to tell you one thing, that I love you, because the next time I see you, you'll be lying in a casket. You won't be able to hear what I have to say. That's why I want you to hear me right now. That's why I want you to know I love you."

I got back in my car drove back to Birmingham. That was all I said to him, but it was less than a week later that Jimmy was in Bradford. I was very skeptical at first. He's B.S.ing everybody, he's not there for the right reasons, and all that. Anyway, he got out after staying for 30 days, and then I thought about those 3 beer joints he owned back in Tuscaloosa. There's no way he can stay sober. Not being around alcohol all the time. But he did. He's a miracle. It's a miracle he's still alive. Thank God !

At one time or another we've all done things that could have put us in the grave. When I speak to these different groups, I'll ask everybody how many of them should be dead right now? There's not a hand in there that doesn't go up. Then I'll ask how many of you have ever been in jail? How many of you ever been fired from a job? How many of you have wrecked 4 or 5 cars? How many have been divorced 3 or 4 times? Everybody is raising their hands. Then I say, I never had any of that. I've never been locked up. Never been put in jail. Never been in a car wreck. Never got in a fight. Never had a DUI, because I saw it all coming. I have been lucky. I have talked my way out of countless DUI's and tickets. But that was just a blessing. That's why I need to hear these stories from these people out here. Stories of wreckin' cars, getting fired, gettin' those handcuffs put on 'em. Chemical dependency does not discriminate. It doesn't care who you are, how much money you got, what color you are, it just doesn't discriminate. I've been very fortunate. I've had good people help guide me and direct me. They let me know what was coming. I was headed downhill fast after my divorce. It could have been so easy for me to take that other road. But there comes a time when you got to decide which way to go. You can go the right way, or you can go that same ol' highway with all its potholes and speed breakers. Once I got on the right road it was amazing how things smoothed out.

I can see where I'm going. I can read the signs. It's just another way of living.

JWH - What was your worst time during your drinking days?

Johnny - Right after my divorce, or during my divorce. I was drinking really heavy, and not staying home. The other day I told somebody , I'm recognized as being one of the outstanding men in Homewood, but 10 years ago I was sleeping in the office and in my car. I look back and I think how sobriety has really turned things around for me. I never hit the kind of bottom where I wound up sleeping under bridges, or in some alley. But I knew it was coming.

After my divorce it was really rough. Being with my wife for 21 years, having two kids, and being successful at just about everything I had done, it was hard for me to accept that I was a failure in my marriage. I had to face the fact that I couldn't be successful at everything, but just knowing I was a failure in my marriage was very hard on me. We had spent tons of money on counseling and therapy. We spent a lot of money trying to solve our problems. We really tried to solve our problems and made a lot of effort to save our marriage. It just didn't work.

One of our marriage counselors told me, "Johnny, you can take 50 per cent of the responsibility for the failure of this marriage, or you can keep on drinking and take 100 per cent. " That's what I was trying to do, take 100 per cent responsibility for the failure of my marriage. But he had also pointed out that maybe I had a drinking problem I needed to work on. That rang my bell for the first time and started me thinking.

JWH - We've talked a lot about alcohol, but did you also do other drugs?

Johnny - No, not really. I did smoke some marijuana, but I didn't like to smoke because I wanted to keep my lungs clear for running. Cold Beer was my drug of choice, and I drank enough of it to kill a 100 people. I like cold beer and what it did to me, and I could control it. At least at first. That control was what got me in trouble and kept me in denial. I could drink beer and go to work. I could drink beer and train. I could drink beer and still out run everybody. I could drink beer and function. At least that's the way I thought at the time. I looked good on the outside, but nobody knows what goes on behind closed doors. I was dying on the inside. People couldn't believe that me and my wife were getting a divorce. They'd say, 'we thought you two were the perfect couple,' but they didn't know. That's the way everybody is, we don't want others to know the truth. We all have secrets. We've all done things we're not proud of, but we can't go back. We can't unring a bell after we've already rung it.

JWH - In my opinion you're a natural born entertainer. When you got a few beers in you that entertainer came out. How has being sober affected that entertainer?

Johnny - We do this Blues Brothers show, and I do some Elvis imitations. I used to get good and loaded before I went on-stage. I remember after I got sober I wondered if I could still do it. Well you know what? I can do it better now that I know what I'm doing. I've got my coordination back. I can move better than the King, or Dan Ackroyd
     One of the best compliments I ever got was when we were playing a sold out show at the Comedy Club. There was this stage manager that told me, "I've been in Los Angeles, Chicago, Hollywood, New York, and I've seen my share of impersonators, but I've never seen anyone do Blues Brothers better than you do. I felt like this was a real compliment coming from an old pro like him. I'm 54 years old, but I'm in the best condition of any 54 year old around.
     I can do it better now because I'm sober, and I'm in great shape. Getting up there on stage and really going after it, knowing it's something you love to do, is really great.
     Entertainment is making folks feel good. I try to be enter-

taining every day, even if it's in the check out line in the Piggly Wiggly store. If I can make that check out girl smile, it's been worth it. Who knows what's going on in her life. She may have an abusive husband. She may have a sick child, or whatever. I'll tell her, "If I hit that 17 million dollar lottery today, I'll buy you a new car costing up to $50,000." That'll bring a smile, or a chuckle or two. For me, I feel I've brightened her day, even if it's just for a moment or two.

I like to have fun. I like to carry on with people. I like standup comedians. I can watch them on TV, and I'll be laughing so hard I'll be down on the floor rolling.

JWH - How did you get involved with the Baby Boomers and the Blues Brothers act?

Johnny - It goes back to when I saw the Blues Brothers on Saturday Night Live. I had liked that show ever since it came on, and I liked Dan Ackroyd because I identified with him. He was tall and slim, and he had athletic moves. When I saw him I knew I could do the moves and the things he did. Well, Suzie and I were going to a Halloween party, and I didn't know what kind of costume to wear, so I decided to go as one of the Blues Brothers; black suit, black hat, and briefcase. We went to some hotel in Birmingham, I forget which one, and I danced every dance at that party and was a big hit.

After that, Eddie Elrod and I started to pantomime the act. We recorded the songs on a ghetto blaster and practiced and practiced. When word got out the phone started ringing off the hook, and we started doing all kinds of parties. Now, every year at the Vulcan Run, we dress up as the Blues Brothers and run the marathon. We cut up all along the way, and then do the awards ceremonies. When people are all standing around, waiting for runners to finish, it is boring, so we keep them entertained and cause some excitement.

Eddie had been in a band earlier on, and just like with the Blues Brothers, they were getting the band back together. The Baby Boomers are a great band. It's a high energy show, and we've got one of the best Elvis imitators in the business. We've done The Comedy Club several times and it has always sold out.

When they dim those house lights and the spotlight goes to the back of the room for our entrance we go through the crowd high-fiving, kissin' the women; and all this time that Blues Brothers beat is playing in the background. And from there on its "high energy." We're flat gettin' after it. We can do it better than the original's because we're in better shape. They smoked and drank and drugged like crazy, but me and Eddie are two of the fittest guys in the world. I used to have to get all boozed up to do it. I know those folks don't have their minds on their troubles. They're happy for a while, and like I said, I like to make folks smile and be happy.

JWH - Where does your entertainer side come from?

Johnny - It comes from being the child of an alcoholic. I wanted to make people laugh and grin. Just let me perform. It didn't matter what-juggle, turn flips, play guitar, anything-just let me perform. That way you want ask me where's your dad, or mom. Are they alcoholics? I wouldn't have to tell you I haven't eaten a meal at home in a week. That all I've had to eat, besides school lunches, is candy out of the store. Just let me keep you entertained, and that way you won't ask me about what goes on after school. I wouldn't have to tell you about mama slapping or beating me; about daddy using a belt or chain to beat me when he was in one of his drunken furies. If I was entertaining you, you wouldn't notice the holes in my socks, or in my coveralls, or my shirts. I remember my brother gave me one of his shirts. It was a Hop-A-Long-Cassidy shirt, and it had sixteen patches on it. I had to wear that shirt to school, and I was so ashamed and embarrassed. That's why I had to be the class clown.

Just let me out at recess and out run everybody. Or let me jump the farthest, or throw the best horseshoes, and that way you wouldn't notice the patches. That's why I loved to play all those games. It was to forget about all the things that were really happening in my life. That's why I like to make people laugh.

But I cried a lot when I was a kid. I will never forget when I was in the 3rd grade at Taylorville Elementary School, and someone came up to me and said, "Your mom is an alcoholic. All she does is lay up drunk." I remember hid-

**Johnny Montgomery
Second Grade**

ing from the other kids and crying my eye's out. It was like someone knew something about me that I didn't want them to know. That made me want to entertain more. Do more, so you couldn't see right through me.

JWH - What about your sisters? Did they have trouble with alcohol, too?

Johnny - Not really. I think the jury might still be out on my older sister. She's pretty hard headed. Of course she knows everything, and if you know everything then no one can tell you anything. I don't know if it's for me to judge. All I know is she likes to have several cold one's at night. She may be in denial, or she may not. I just hope and pray that she's not. If she is I hope one day she finds what me and Jimmy got.

JWH - How's your relationship with your kids?

Johnny - Meridith is 23 now and she's in college. Megan is 12 and she'll be going into 7th grade. I've got two of the best girls in the world. I am so fortunate. I've been blessed. I shouldn't complain about anything. I mean I really shouldn't. I've been blessed with a job I really like doing. I have two daughters that's crazy about me. I'm so very blessed. For the last nine years I've been in a program that let's me know that I know there's a Higher Power that's going to take care of me. Things happen that aren't luck. Once you get out of the grip of chemical dependency you realize there is a Higher Power. You want to know more about this Power. You read more, you study more, there's a hunger for knowledge about this side of your life.

I started going to church in these last nine years. I go to Dawson Memorial Baptist Church, and Gary Finton is my pastor. One day in the past year I went over to his office. I was having trouble with a relationship that was just ending. I told him I've got to get rid of some pain. I'm ready to surrender. He asked if I had ever been saved. I told him I hadn't. I got down on my knee's and I gave my life to Jesus that day. It's amazing the peace that came over me.

That day when I left, I got in my car and I knew something had happened to me, but I said, "God, where are you? I felt something, but God, where are you?" That's the part of faith that you've got to really believe. I had a 6:30 appointment, and this is in January, and I'm going down Highway 280. Traffic was backed up, it was dark, and the clock in my Cadillac had been broken for about a year. It was like a microwave oven when the power goes off and it's locked at 12:00 o'clock. I took it to the Crest Cadillac dealership and they said they would have to order the parts and it would take 4 or 5 weeks for them to come in. They ordered the parts, but I never had the time to go there and let them fix it, so my clock had been locked at 12 O'clock all that time. Anyway, I'm feeling God's peace, and I'm driving down 280 and I'm thinking I'm going to be late for my 6:30 appointment. I look at my watch and it reads 6:08. I look at that broken clock in my car and it read 6:08 ! Now if that don't get your attention, nothing will. I kept watching that clock, 6:09, 6:10., then on and on. I pulled into the parking lot at 6:25. I cut the car off, went in, showed this house that took about 45 minutes, came back out, turned the car on and the clock is back at 12:00. We can go out in the garage right now and that clock will be on 12:00. I've heard burning bush stories, but of course they're always someone else's story. And I know that once you start getting some faith people want to put you into that category with snake handlers and poison drinkers, and I'm not into any of that. I think I'm just a simple believer, but it was something that day that I needed. And God fills all our needs. How that clock came back on I don't know, and it hasn't been back on since.

But that's kind of the way my life has been. That's part of having the trust and faith to get you through the trials and tribulations of everyday life. God gives us the strength not to just go nuts, or get all excited. Not that I don't get excited sometimes, but then I find that peace and calm down. I know everything is going to be O.K. Life is fairly simple. It's us that's makes it complicated.

JWH - Your pastor lead you to the peace and serenity that only Jesus can give. Your pastor seems to be the one person that inspired your new life.

Johnny - Yea, he's a huge inspiration to me. In fact I started seeing him on TV years ago, when I was going to another church. It was a small community church. It was like going from the minor leagues to the major leagues. I needed more, I wanted more. In fact, I had seen Gary when he had first come to Dawson years ago. We were sitting in New York Pizza having a beer with Jerry Fitzgerald, a buddy of mine, who turned around and said here's the new preacher. I looked at him and he looked at me and there was a chemistry there. Even though

I didn't talk to him 'till 3 or 4 years later when I decided to visit over there, I'd see him around Homewood all the time, and there was always something there. The day when I did visit, when I walked into Dawson Memorial, I knew I was home. That was 5 years ago, and I've been there ever since. Anytime I need anything, he's always there. He gives me that reassurance that everything's going to be O.K., everything is going to be fine. When you hear his message you hear the things you need to know, right now, regardless of what your situation is.

Even back when I would see him on TV he would say something that I needed to hear. And then it just snowballed and I had to see this guy in person.

JWH - Do you read your Bible everyday?

Johnny - Yes I do, and it's having an amazing effect. The hunger you get. The wanting to know more. Once these things start happening to you, you know there's more to life than just cars, houses, and work. There's a peace. You open the Bible up and you find that peace. Right now, where I am in my life is Psalm 18:32, "[It is] God that girdeth me with strength, and maketh my way perfect." Man, it's wild for Johnny Montgomery to be quoting scripture verses.

I was down in Panama City doing a triathlon, and we had to swim one and a half miles in the Gulf. The day before the race the water looked like glass. The day of the race the water was white capping. The conditions were horrible. The Lord put Psalm 18:32 in my head, and I knew he was going to protect me and give me strength and surefootedness. I knew he was going to protect me from those waves. He's going to give me strength for my body to swim through those waves. Strength to swim those one and a half miles, then jump onto a bicycle and peddle 56 miles, and then jump off and run 13 miles more. So I had a peace and comfort with me. Now, a few years back I would have been the one biting my fingernails, and I might not have got into that ocean. But this day I never batted an eye. I knew everything would be all right. I knew I wasn't going to drown. I knew he was going to take care of me. I was literally walking up and down the beach having to calm my fellow swimmers. Some were getting hysterical. Anyway, when they shot the starting gun a lot of people went into that water, but a lot of them couldn't get over those waves. They got knocked back up on the beach with their goggles knocked off, crying, really scared., I was walking up and down the beach saying,

"Hey, everything is going to be O.K. God's going to take care of us. Nobody has ever drowned before, and your not going to drown." It was amazing. People said to me, Johnny, thanks for talking to me, I really needed that, and I really appreciate you. The next thing you know, people are in that water taking off. Taking off to race! Psalms really helped me to help them that day. God works that way, you know.

JWH - Were you an appliance salesman before you got into real estate? I've heard some wild stories about you as the super salesman.

Johnny - I worked for W.T. Grants. One day a blind lady came in. She had been blind all her life, and I sold her a T.V. Not just a black and white set, but a top of the line color T.V. Another time I sold a washer and dryer to a couple that didn't even have indoor plumbing. We had to repossess that set 3 months later. When the movers went to pick them up they said they had to shoo the chickens off the washer and dryer that was still sitting on their front porch where they had originally delivered them.

JWH - How long did you work for W.T. Grants?

Johnny - I was with them from 1972 to 1977. When I moved to Birmingham I was going to coach and teach. They were going to pay me $6000 a year. I took a job with W.T. Grants to supplement my income. I made $10,000 in 3 months selling televisions, stereos, washers and dryers, and other appliances. I took my shoes off and started adding things up. I made 5 F's in college Math, but I figured out I needed to stay in sales, and I wound up being the top salesman in the nation for them.

Those days got me ready for the sales I do today. My sales today are mainly repeats and referrals. There's very few that ever do business with me that don't come back again. I've built up a great relationship with those I do business with.

When I was with W.T. Grant, they wanted everybody to have a charge card. They would give us salesmen a silver dollar for every application we turned in. On Saturday morning I couldn't walk back to my car at lunch time for all the silver dollars I was carrying. My competitive nature, being what it is, took me into that contest to win.

But then they went bankrupt. I wondered what I was going to do then. I could go to work with Sears, Pennys, Riches, or wherever, but then I thought about it. I liked to play baseball and run races, both of which took place on Saturday's. And Saturday was retails biggest day. You got to be there when the store opens on Saturday morning if you want to make any money. I thought about real estate. It was 100% commission, so if I worked hard I would make a lot of money, and if I wanted to play I could go play. I decided to get into real estate, thinking it would be easy. I never dreamed it would be as hard as it is.

I didn't even have a car. My first year I sold a million dollars worth of real estate from my pick up truck. But I think the real reason I tried so hard was because I thought I would have to go back to work if I didn't succeed. And it has turned out very well for me. I've sold over a million every year since I've been in real estate, and of course I'm a multi-million producer.

JWH - Who were your mentors in the real estate business?

Johnny - Bill Waldrop was my mentor. He's one of my partners now. When I first got my license and got into real estate, I thought I had the attitude of the real estate world. World, here I am, come and get me! Well, Bill would come up missing for a week or two, and here I am wandering around in this office that was about the size of a phone booth, wondering, where is he? What do I do now?

He would finally show up and answer my questions, and it then began to dawn on me. Real estate is one of those businesses where you either sink or swim. You have to get out there and go. That was what he was doing. It was the answer to the one question I never had to ask because he showed me. First you sell all your friends a house, then you turn lose on the world. Just like an insurance salesman. And like I said, me and Bill have been partners since 1979.

JWH - Tell me of some of your successes in the real estate business.

Johnny - Making the million dollar club my first year was a really big deal. Back then, making the million dollar club was really something. Then in the late 70's and early 80's when interest rates jumped up to 17 or 18% a lot of agents got out of the business because of the really tight market. But I didn't. I stayed with it through those really tough years, and I stayed in the million or multi-million dollar club that whole time. I've been one of the top producers in Birmingham ever since I've been in real estate. That's something I'm proud of. I'm pretty well known, and everyone says they like to do business with me. I guess my good reputation is my proudest achievement.

JWH - Why you and not that guy down the street?

Johnny - Honesty and sincerity. I think when I sit down with somebody to deal with them on their investment, whether it's $35,000 or $500,000, the amount doesn't matter, I treat their money just like it was mine. I don't do the gotcha's, surprises, or gouges. I don't miss their monthly payment amount by $300 a month, or if I tell them their closing cost will be $3500, it will more likely be $3200, not $5000. In these days if you start making mistakes with other people's money you're going to get a bad reputation. It comes down to, yes, your going to sell that house, but they'll go tell all their friends. If you do them a good job, they will tell them that, but if you do them a bad job they'll go tell that about twice as fast and twice as loud. I want people to tell their friends, 'When you want real estate, call Johnny.' Like I said, the bottom line is honesty and sincerity.

My real secret is product knowledge. If somebody wants something particular, I have to know where to find it. If they have something for sale, I have to know how and to who to sell it to. I'm a problem solver and information broker.

JWH - What's your advice to anyone going into the real estate business?

Johnny - Real estate is a really deceiving business. I'm what you call a lazy workaholic. A lot of people see me doing what I do, and I make it look really easy because I'm good at it. Anyway, they look at me and say, if Johnny can do that I can do that. And they can't. It's like watching golf on T.V., they make it look real easy, but most people can't do it like the pro's.

People pay for my knowledge. I sell a ton of 'For Sale by Owners,' properties. They could do the same thing I do. They can market the house just as well. They can put ad's in the paper and open their doors to the public for showing. They can fluff the goods, put smell good in there, but they can't close. It's very hard for them to ask the customer, "How much money do you have? Have you ever been in debtor's court? Are you paying alimony and/or child support? What is your car worth?" They can't ask those personal things.

When I bring somebody over to see the house, they are

fully qualified. I'll know before hand if they have enough money, and if their credit is good. The person that puts a 'For Sale by Owner' sign in his front yard has no way of knowing all this. They've got to let anybody come into their home. The next guy to drive up might be Charles Manson, but if he wants to see your house you've got to show it to him.

I also see a lot of this. The husband puts up a 'For Sale by Owner' sign in the yard. Now, this guy works for a big company and is out of town a lot. When he's out of town, he's going to leave his wife and kids to open up the house to anybody that cares to show up. With all the stuff going on these days I really don't think most people would want that. In fact I think it's a downright stupid thing to do.

It's like if your having a heart attack, do you want that guy down at the Shell station working on it? No, you want the best heart doctor you can find working on it. It's the same in real estate. Do you really want to hammer up a sign in your front yard and trust yourself to handle all the intricacies of the deal, or do you want me, a qualified agent, to handle all those details? Do you want me to get you the most money for your property, with the least amount of hassle and surprises? Do you want it done right?

When I go to a 'For Sale by Owner' property, I don't go in and beg him to let me sell their house. I never say a word about selling the house. I just look at the property and chat with them about their needs. But I always carry a long list of people looking for houses in certain area's or certain price ranges, and if anything matches up I let them know I may have someone interested in buying from them.

I just let those people see me. I don't try to put them under any pressure. I'm not out there trying to cram an elephant into a Volkswagen, and I think they see that. They see I'm a professional, and they think, 'This guy really knows what he's talking about.' They know I know how to get them to the finish line in their real estate needs.

JWH - How do you see the real estate industry changing?

Johnny - It has changed so much just since I've been in the business. Me and Joe Mizerany, another of my mentors, were the first one's in this business to have car phones. That was back when they were around $400 a month. I guess we were just a little ahead of our time. And just look what fax machines and computers have done in the last few years. Now everybody has a cellular phone, and most everybody has a computer. Now we can handle so much more business so much more quickly. It's just amazing. I remember when I first got into the business all those older realtors never would change with the times. They opposed the Multiple Listings Book, and any other new techniques that came out. I was like one of those proverbial ol' dogs that wouldn't learn any new tricks when computers first started coming out. But I knew if I was going to stay successful I had to stay on top of things. I'm not going to be out high-teched by anyone. I've got a computer on my desk here at home and three at the office. The only thing I don't have is a laptop computer. I don't see the need for one of those right now, but you can bet if I did, I'd have one.

There's all kind of changes going on. In the future their may not be a mortgage banker involved. Their role might be taken over by computers. Your credit could be approved over the computer, without all the hassles we go through now. The same might be true of title work or surveys. Everything is getting quicker.

JWH - Real estate seems to always be increasing in price. Will this trend continue?

Johnny - I've been selling real estate for 22 years, and that question is asked everyday. How can this house be worth more next year? Now we're talking prime location. That's the determining factor, location, location, location. In a neighborhood like Homewood, AL. the prices will keep on inflating. You can go outside in the street and watch them inflate. I've never seen them not inflate. They may slow down when interest rates go up, but the prime area's of investment always go up. Say a house cost $450,000. Will that house be worth a million in ten years? Generally speaking, they double in price about every ten years, so, yes it would. I don't see this trend stopping in any of the prime area's.

I saw a newspaper printed in 1932. In the real estate section the homes in Homewood and Mountain Brook were the highest in price. If you look at the price of those same homes today, it's unbelievable. It makes you want to buy all the real estate you can get your hands on in prime area's. At the time you may think, 'Oh no, I've got to pay market value for this,' but a year later you'll be thinking, 'Oh man, I really stole this place.' I have yet to have anyone lose a nickel on a house in a prime area.

JWH - What should the average person NOT DO in real estate?

Johnny - They should never NOT use a Realtor. That Realtor knows the business. That Realtor knows what's going on. And not just in one section of town, but all over town as a whole. That Realtor knows what's happening now, what's happened in the past, and what's likely to happen in the future. It's changing everyday. Values are continuing to go up, technology is changing, and that Realtor knows these changes. First, he knows the areas NOT to buy in, and the areas TO buy in. So, if I could give everybody some real sound advice it would be to get yourself a Realtor if your going to buy real estate.

If you've got a legal problem, call a lawyer. If you have an accounting problem, call an accountant. If your sick, go to a hospital, but if you have a real estate problem, call a Realtor.

JWH - Tell us about Johnny, the coach.

Johnny - I started running by myself, and it was like people came running like chicks running to a hen. So I started coaching in 1972. I've coached people that are now scattered all over the world. I get cards from California, New York, Switzerland; all over. They say my folks are the best bunch of runners that run all over the world for different track clubs and groups, and countries. They say there's none better than the one's I've coached.

I always make my track team do what I call "dessert." Whenever they get through with their workout I'll say, "Ya'll come on, we're going to run one more mile, or half mile, or whatever, and were going to hammer it." That's what I call "dessert."

Well, a friend of mine, Kazi, flew in from Switzerland about 8 years ago for training, and he still tells this story. I called for "dessert." He said in broken English he was thinking, "Johnny, you run our butts off. You almost run us to death, and then you tell us to get out on the starting line for 'dessert.' I think to myself, Why are we going to start eating on the race track this early in the day. Then I find out what 'Dessert' is when you made me run another mile. I almost died." He said, "Now that I'm coaching runners in Switzerland I make them do "dessert" everyday. Just like you do, Johnny."

Kazi is a baker. Bruno's brought him over here to teach them how to make pastries and cakes, and all that stuff. He was over here about 3 years, and when I coached him he ran races all over the South. He's a great runner. I gave him and Oxford running shirt and he framed it. It's hanging in his house over there. That's how much he thought of us over here.

JWH - What does it take to be a great runner?

Johnny - If your going to have a chicken salad sandwich, there's got to be a little bit of chicken in there somewhere. You've got to have a little bit of talent, and then it's who wants it the most. Sure, when you shoot the gun, and these people run the 100 yard dash, that's a natural gift of God. That's a God given talent. But then to take that on to the 400, 800, mile, 2 miles, or 26 mile mark, that's when the real blue collar class people come in. That's because you've really got to work for that. Sure, you've got to have talent, but what it come down to is who's got the hunger. Who's willing to work the hardest to get what they want. It's that personal drive inside that determines who wins. It's just that simple.

JWH - What does it take to run an Ironman? Can you go back to that first day and tell me what it was like ?

Johnny - Yea. I saw a guy on T.V. once that said the Ironman was the toughest event in the world, and I knew right then that's what I wanted to do. That was in 1980. In 1984 I had my first shot at the Ironman in Hawaii. I can't tell you the feeling of being in the water with 1500 of the best athletes world. T.V. cameras from every country were rolling, taking it all in. I never got to compete in the Olympics, and I never played for a championship team, but I was here and this was the world championships. That ain't too bad for an ol' uneducated country boy that used to swim in cow ponds.

The Ironman competition consists of a 2.4 mile ocean swim, a 112 mile bike ride through the lava fields, and a 26 mile run. I told someone in another interview that the Ironman is like committing suicide with a toothbrush. It's a slow death. You know your going to die, it's just a matter of when. You get into the ocean and you swim until you die, then you swim another mile and a half. Then you get onto the bike and ride for five hard hours and die, and then you ride another hour. Then you run until you die, and then you run another 10 miles. The first time I went, I had no idea how grueling it would be. If I could have quit I would have.

Number one, I had never swam that far in my life. Number 2, I had never had 1500 other swimmers swimming all around and even across me. It was like a catfish feeding frenzy.

After I got out about a mile and a half, I got severe leg cramps in my legs, calves, and feet. I had to flip over in the water to shake off the cramps, and I knew I was in some seriously deep water. Like I said, I would have quit if I could have, but that meant someone from shore would have to come get me. All I could think was to keep going and going, because I was fairly certain that no one on the bank would come and get my country butt.

The cramps were starting to move up my body, and I started fearing for my life. When the cramps move up that high, and you can't move anymore, that's when you can drown. The pain was so bad that drowning seemed like it was the easy way out. I have no idea how I made it. I just kept going and going until I finished. I found out later that I swam it in an hour and 37 minutes. That's along time to be out in the open ocean.

Then came the bicycles. This was in the days before titanium, the aero bars, and all the speed stuff we've got now. But

I got on that bike and took off. The first 50 miles the wind was in our face. It was blowing so strong in some places you had to stand up to bike downhill. Then on the way back the cramps started in again because I hadn't eaten or drank enough beforehand. My shoulders felt like they were going to fall off. The pavement was about 112 degree's because it was laid directly over lava rock with no trees or shade of any kind around. It took 7 hours and 40 minutes to finish that bike race. Now Jerry, that's a long time to be straddle that bike seat. It's about the size of a banana. Think about that for awhile.

And then I had to take off running. Or, I should say, I took off on the "Death March," since it was a 26 mile run. There was some sad singin' and slow walkin' going on about that time. The physical end of it was gone for me. My body was shutting down. There was nothing left except my will to finish that race.

I have never been a quitter. From bailing hay on the farm, to that day at the Ironman, I have never been a quitter. I just had to finish. Call it my will, call it whatever, but I knew I just had to finish. It took everything in me to finish. There were bodies on both sides of the road, and the Medical tent at the finish line looked like the railroad yard scene out of "Gone with the Wind." If you've ever seen a race on T.V. like this, with people literally crawling over the finish line and collapsing, then you know what I'm talking about. They will tell you your a winner for just crossing that line. That gives you the will, the determination to put everything you've got into it just to cross that finish line.

Later, as my sobriety got stronger, I took from that. It was not just one day at a time, but 1 mile at a time. Whatever it took. Whatever you've got to do to survive while your out there, that's what you do. It's unbelievable what the human body will endure.

The crowd over there is special. When your coming down Ali Drive, they could take a chain saw and cut both your legs off and you'd still have to run to the finish line on your nubs because that crowd want let you quit. It's like the Gladiators from back in Roman days. After each conquest the crowd would cheer them on. As I crossed that finish line I knew that there were very few people in the world that could do this. After my 8th competition I knew that there were very few people in the world that had done it 8 times. I'm the only man from Alabama that's done it 8 times, and that does set me apart from the average person, but I am not the greatest triathlete in the world.

JWH - Seems God takes that trip with you. Do you pray during those hard times?

Johnny - Psalms 18:32 says God girdeth me with strength, and makes my way perfect, and I know God gives me strength and protects me. He didn't leave me out there in that ocean for a shark to eat, or to drown. After the gas tank is gone and the nook is passed the peg, then God keeps you going. It's God. It ain't me. That poem, "Footprints in the Sand," that's what God does. He carries me through tough times. Every time I've called on him, he's delivered, and not let me down. Whatever I've achieved it's because of my Higher Power.

JWH - Do you want to tell us anymore about your higher power ?

Vulcan 10K Run - 1984

Johnny - Yes. I'd just like to tell everyone, trust Him. Life is simple. It's us that get it all complicated. We all have fears and character defects, but they can be controlled regardless of what they are. That's why the liquor stores can be full of liquor, and the drug stores full of drugs, and it don't bother me. Sooner or later everyone has to face up to their real problems, and when they figure out you've got to turn it over to God things start to get better.

One of my daily prayers is, "God, it's between you and me. I can't handle it alone, but with you, we can handle any thing." It might not always be pretty, and it may be a little ragged around the edges sometimes, but I never loss sight of the fact that He is always with me. I'm in this house by myself, and sometimes I get lonely. But I always know that I'm never alone.

JWH - I heard you ran a race after a bad bike accident once. Tell me about that.

Johnny - In August of '97 after I had already qualified for the October Hawaiian Ironman, I was on a hundred mile bike ride. I had done about 70 miles by myself when a bunch of buddies came out to keep me company. Another buddy of mine had qualified, and wanted to get in on some long rides. We were out on Lakeshore Parkway in Birmingham doing about 28 miles per hour. I'll never forget the speed because I had just looked down at my speedometer and it read 28 miles per hour. I had never had a bike accident in my life because I'm an excellent biker and always bike with the same group of guys because you can anticipate what they are going to do. Well, we had a new guy with us, Bruce Gennari. He was a big ol' guy, about 6'6" and it seemed like he created a bigger vacuum, like the NASCAR guys do at Talledega, because of his extreme size. I already had 70 or so miles under my belt, and I was thinking about food. I was thinking, I'm going to eat grits, bacon, Spam and eggs, anything I can get my hands on after we finish biking, when my front tire got sucked into his rear tire and in a situation like this whoever is in the rear is going to go down. I did go down. Hard. And I knew this wasn't good. It felt like I had broken every rib in my body and I couldn't move a muscle. I kept thinking, "I've worked so hard to get the Ironman slot, and they're so tough to get. Now I've blown it." They called an ambulance and as they hauled me away to Brookwood hospital I ran my fingers down my shirt and I could feel my collar bone and ribs all crumbled up. I knew that wasn't the way the Lord had put me together. When I got to the hospital they found a broken collar bone, which was doing everything but sticking out through my skin. They also found two broken ribs and a punctured lung, which was causing me to breath at about one tenth my lung capacity. At Brookwood all I could think about was how the Ironman was out for me that year. It was only 6 weeks away, but then I got to thinking, maybe I could bike, maybe I could run. But with the collar bone broken I knew swimming was out. I had to be crazy, because I was thinking all this in the ICU.

After I got out of the hospital I couldn't even get out of bed on my own. I had to have people help me to the bathroom. I couldn't feed myself, and I was in extreme pain. About a week later the newspaper reported that I was injured and wouldn't be in the Ironman that year. The newspaper said I was too broke up to go, and everyone else was saying the same thing. But that was my decision, and I hadn't thrown in the towel just yet. Even though I didn't look good, I knew that there may not be another chance for me at the Ironman, so I started going to the pool and training. The first day all I could take was 5 minutes and it was on the way back home for me. Then about a week later I could actually walk. In another week I had folks helping me onto my bike and I would go up and down Lakeshore Parkway. The first day I couldn't change gears, so I just stayed in first gear and did 20 miles. Then I figured that if I could do 20 that day then all I needed to do was pick it up another 85 or 90 miles before the triathlon. When they took me to Health South for rehabilitation I couldn't even lift my arm, so they put a drawstring on it where I could pull it up and down. And then it was back at the pool where I was finally able to swin a whole lap. That seemed like the greatest of things then, so I took it own myself to swim another 25 yards. Now all I had to figure out was how to go another 2.4 miles, so I went back the next day and swam 200 yards, and the next day and swam 400 yards. That's when I said, yep, I'm going to the Ironman.

It got to where I could do 50 miles on the bike, and change gears. Then my swimming got up to a mile, but I could only run 10 miles and I didn't know if I could increase that to 26 miles before the event or not. I ended up going to that Ironman. I prayed that my Lord would give me the strength, because I didn't have any. I told him, "I don't have it, so you've got to do it for me."

When the gun shot, I was the last one in the water. I didn't want to take any chance that someone would hit my broken collar bone. It's still not right. It flops around like a windshield wiper to this very day. But once I got into the water, I found a comfortable motion. Where normally I would swim it in an hour and 15 to 20 minutes, I swam it in an hour and 25 minutes. It was amazing.

Then I got on the bike. Everything was going pretty good up until the last 40 miles. That's when I got into a real stiff wind. Every muscle in my body was hurting. I can't begin to put

into words the way my collar bone felt. I was doing everything
with my legs, and it seems like it took me 7 and a half hours to
finish that bike ride. It was a brutal, brutal event, but then on
the run I got to thinking I could finish it under 17 hours. If you
win the Ironman medal, everybody knows you're alive. If you
don't finish in less than 17 hours, nobody even knows you've

been there. I walked the first two miles, and it took me 26 minutes. I knew if I kept up that pace it would take me another 19 hours to finish the race, so I decided I've got to get going. I've got to get going now! I started jogging, and I jogged, and I jogged. I wound up doing it in something like 14 and a half hours. I thank God for that victory. He was with me every step of the way, and I knew with Jesus at my side, he helped me finish with 2 and a half hours to spare! Looking back now, I feel like I was on a mission from God.

God let me know I could do it. I've been there 8 times and I've gotten 8 medals. The next time I'm going for the win. God let me know I can do it. I don't need another finishers medal. The next time I'm going for the winners medal.

Jimmy Montgomery
Brother
Bar Owner

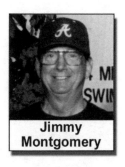

Jimmy
Montgomery

JWH - Jimmy, could you describe Johnny in one paragraph?

Jimmy - Of course. I'm prejudiced because he's my brother, but I think Johnny is one of the finest human beings that I've ever known. He's honest, he's dedicated to his family, his training, and his God. Johnny is a true Christian. He's somebody that I look up to, and I couldn't ask for a better brother. I love him and I try to tell him that I'm so proud of him.. With Johnny, what you see is what you get.

JWH - Tell us about growing up.

Jimmy - We grew up in that old country store. This was during the time when Mom and Pop grocery stores were on their way out because the big stores took all the profit from that type of small business. We grew up in an alcoholic atmosphere. Some of my earliest memories are the times when daddy would come home late at night drunk and want to kill all of us. We would have to hide in the bedroom and put the furniture up against the door to keep him out, and all night long we would be scared to death that daddy would somehow break in and kill us. We went through these things, and then would have to go to school the next day.

Our parents got divorced in 1950, when I was 12 or 13, and Johnny was somewhere around 5 years old. Daddy moved about a mile down the road, and mama and us stayed there at the store. Johnny and I, as well as our two sisters, had a tough life back then. Our oldest sister Jeanette missed a lot of it because she was old enough to leave home by the time we came

First Swimming Pool - 1950

around. But our mama never drank during all the years that they were married. After the divorce daddy kept on drinking, and that was when mama started drinking. Mother's drinking eventually got worse than daddy's. We all grew up in that drinking atmosphere. That's the only life we knew since we were bootleggers and sold whiskey. Johnny and I have poured up as much moonshine whiskey as anybody, and I've drank many a gallon myself.

We grew up in a family where our mama and daddy never said that they loved us, or that they were proud of what we were doing. It was like whatever you did was not good enough, and I think they instilled the attitude in us that we weren't as good as other people.

None of us got much of an education. Our parents weren't educated, so they saw little need in it for us either. They put all their effort into making money and they chased the almighty dollar all of their lives. They owned a good bit of property, too. But even with all that, they did teach us some good things. We were taught to be honest, to be fair, and to try to make your word your bond. I remember daddy used to tell us that a Montgomery didn't have to lie or steal. Now don't get me wrong. Our lives weren't all bad, there were some good times, too.

Johnny went through grammar and high school without missing one day. That was quite a feat because with a mama like ours, it could be rough. Mama would more than likely be drunk, and we had to get ourselves up and off to school. Not that mama stayed drunk all the time, but she would hit these periods of time where she was totally non-functional. Once mama got to drinking, she was a rough, mean person. She shot at Johnny with a pistol, once. And she shot at me a few times, too. When she got half-lit she got mean.

Of course, we grew up in that store where you had to be tough at times. That store never had a license the whole time it was open, and a bootleggers biggest day was Sunday, so a license wouldn't have done us any good anyway. About once a year the Sheriff's Department would come when the Sheriff needed to get his name in the paper, or there would be a complaint, or whatever. I remember one experience from our bootlegging days when the sheriff's department paid us a visit. We knew in advance that they were coming, because we had friends down at the Courthouse. We always knew, and we would be ready for them.

Back then Johnny already ran everyday, and to keep his feet in good shape he used a lot of foot powder. He kept it in a beer box. It was a white powder, and he would put a tray full of this powder on the floor and stand in it to get the powder all over his feet. The day they raided us mama just sat behind the counter as usual, and kept quiet. She acted like she was watching T.V., but I knew she was mad as hell. These detectives came up behind the counter and found Johnny's box of powder. One of them would stick his finger in it and then lick his finger. Then the other one would stick his finger in and lick it. I guess they thought they had found a beer box full of cocaine, or something. The head guy said, "Mrs. Montgomery, what is this?" Mama said, "I don't know, it is something for my son's feet when they get all hot and sweaty. I think it's some kind of foot powder." Those detectives started looking a little green around the gills and just turned around and high-tailed it out of there without saying another word.

Back then was when Johnny really got into running. Running became his life. He ran everyday, and he still does. Johnny's 53 now, and he still builds his day around running. He's very dedicated to it.

JWH - Do you remember Johnny's college days?

Jimmy - Red Drew was the coach at the University of Alabama, and he gave Johnny a scholarship. Johnny didn't pass the entrance exam at Bama, so he went on to Livingston University. They call it West Alabama University now. He got the first track scholarship they ever gave.

Johnny ran the decathlon, which is a 10 event deal. He ran that in high school, and college. Back in high school Johnny finished 3rd in the state in the decathlon. One of the two guys that beat him was Richard Flowers who went on to play some great football for Tennessee.

After Johnny graduated from Livingston he got a job with the W.T. Grant stores. Unless I'm mistaken, Johnny became the leading salesman for the whole corporate system. Any selling contest they ever had, Johnny always won. Always. I joke with Johnny, telling him he was the reason Grant's went broke because they had to pay him so much. When they went bankrupt they owed Johnny for several vacations. He's just a super salesman.

He went on to marry a fine lady by the name of Susie Luxich, and then he got into real estate. He worked for the Oxford Realty Company, and ended up going into partnership with them. Oxford has gone through some tough times, but overall I think they've done really well, and is one of the best companies in Birmingham, Alabama.

I got Johnny in the Guard. All I can say is, Johnny was not a star troop. He and Mickey Nix did nothing but cut up every time we had a meeting. One weekend we were to sleep in pup tents, and Mickey and Johnny and Jerry Latham combined their tents and made this huge shelter that they were all lying

In The National Guard - 1966

under. At inspection time somebody yelled, "Attention!" They kept on lying there, and just stiffened up into their attention pose. There they were, lying there on their backs at attention, and saluting. I was the commander of the unit so and I asked them what all this mess was about. They went into this spiel like, "This is the carport, this is the living room, this is the den." They were giving me a tour of the "quarters".

Then later during the parade, out of 200 Guardsmen there were two wearing sunglasses, which was forbidden. Of course it was Johnny and Mickey. I ended up having to bust my own brother. The worst part was telling mama that there was going to be less pay in that Guard envelope she received every month. She really gave me hell about that.

Another time I remember using Johnny as a lookout. We had some pretty girls down in our rental houses, and one day mama had to go into town. I was lucky enough to have the companionship of one of these fine young ladies that day, so I took her upstairs to my bedroom. I told Johnny to watch for mama. He was to watch the store, but more importantly he was to watch for mama. He got to doing something and wasn't paying attention when mama pulled up, parked, and walked into the store before he ever realized it. He came running to the back of the store hollering up the stairs, "Jimmy, here's mama!" I jumped up and got my clothes back on, but that girl was standing at the top of the stairs with her clothes under her arm, naked as a jay bird, when mama came around the corner and saw her. Mama gave me hell about that, too.

JWH - What was Johnny's influence in your sobering up?

Jimmy - Johnny saw my problem a long, long time before I did. He said a lot of prayers for me, and would try to talk to me, but I didn't see anything wrong with my drinking. I just thought it was a way of life. There, in the last part of my drinking, I was drinking 2 quarts a day and I still didn't think I had a problem. As a matter of fact, I didn't know Johnny had a problem either. He was a beer drinker, and I never considered beer an adult beverage. I always thought it took the hard stuff to get the job done on a real man.

Everybody around me knew I had a drinking problem except me. Alcoholics think that their drinking affects only themselves. Actually, it affects everybody around them in one way or another. I think the biggest mistake I made was thinking that since I was making a living for my family, why should they bother me? Just leave me alone and let me drink was my way of thinking. Thank God Johnny could see my problems, and he never gave up on me. He was a major force in my decision to stop drinking. He finally got through to me and made me realize I was at my bottom. I had to get to the point where I was sick and tired of being sick and tired. Johnny loved me enough not to give up, and I love him for that.

JWH - Jimmy, what were some of the bars you owned?

Jimmy - The first one I owned was primarily a black club called The Diplomat. I had a partner named Nick Armstrong, who became a big man in the night club business back in the 60's. The Diplomat was a place where both blacks and whites were coming. The powers-that-be, or the city fathers, or whoever, didn't like that one little bit. They didn't want blacks and whites getting together. You've got to remember, this was Alabama in the 60's. They shot me down because they had the power. My attorney, Richard Shelby, went to Montgomery to appear before the ABC Board on my behalf. One of the policemen that testified said they had gone into my club and seen a white woman sitting between two black men. And for this they canceled my license.

After that, I went to Northport and bought the DelRue from Pete Pappas. Then I took over Frank's from Bob Bailey. Frank's had been called several different things before, like The Barnhop, and Brothers. And then I bought the place called Little Cookie Restaurant on University Boulevard. That was in 1974, and I've had that bar ever since. It's called The Wooden Door.

I had a friend named Carl Hollihand and he had some cousins, Charlie and Wyman Beck, who were partners with Harry Hammond and someone else. They owned The Brass Monkey on the Strip at the U of A. They weren't getting along, so they came to me and I bought them out. My son Tony helped run that place for awhile, but when the drinking age changed from 19 to 21, it killed The Brass Monkey for me.

I also bought the old Jerry's Drive-In down on 10th Street. It was called Two Ladies for awhile. Then I bought Stax on the Strip. Right now I'm doing good with some other investments I've made, and I'm seriously thinking of getting out of the bar business. I've got three bars now, and I can't be at all of them at the same time. If I'm at one, the other two need me. It's really a strain on my time and energy.

JWH - When you go into one of your bars these days, do you look at them differently than in the days when you were drinking?

Jimmy - I don't have the desire to sit there and listen to the same story 10 times from some drunk. I'd rather spend my time speaking to people who are trying to get away from the ill effects of alcohol. Johnny and I speak to a lot of alcohol recovery groups, and one of the main questions they always ask me is, "How do you sell people whiskey knowing what it did to you?" I tell them that everyone who has a drink doesn't become an alcoholic. I tell them that everyone that sells cars doesn't do so thinking everyone they sell a car to will all be in a head-on collision. I don't feel bad about selling it to people. There's some that are going to take it to extremes like Johnny and I did, and I don't like to see that. I know these people are suffering. Their families are suffering. But one thing I have learned is that I can't fix people. If that drunk don't want a different life, you or I can sit there all day and night and talk to him and all we are doing is wasting our breath. I have learned from Johnny to let go and let God do it. He's teaching me, and he helps me so much.

I know Johnny would do anything for me, now. He's doing good, and is able to help a lot more people, but I don't think he's ever been up to his full potential. Although lately he seems to be steam-rolling a little more. Looks like he's got that snow-ball effect going.

Johnny is somebody special. He is well liked, and people like to be around him. When he goes into a room full of people he becomes the center of attention because he doesn't insult you or talk down to you. He likes to joke and carry on, but not at someone else's expense. He is a caring person, and he always looks for the best in people. He finds it, too. When I'm down, Johnny reminds me of where we have been, and where we are going. He stays focused, and is disciplined and well organized. People sense that. He was honored as Man of the Year in Homewood a few years back. He really is my hero.

JWH - You and Johnny seem to have reversed roles. Early on, you were the father figure. Now he seems to have taken on that role.

Jimmy - I did look on Johnny as a son at times when we were younger. But these days, Johnny is my role-model. He has put our past behind and moved on. He doesn't forget the past, just leaves it where it belongs. Johnny looks for the good things in life each day.

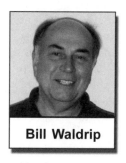

Bill Waldrip

Bill Waldrip
Henry Drake
Partners
Oxford Realty

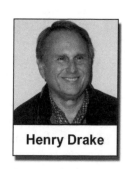

Henry Drake

JWH - How long have you been partners with Johnny?

Bill - About 20 years.

Henry - Maybe more.

Bill - Wasn't it in '78 or '79?

Henry - Somewhere around then.

Bill - We're not great record keepers.

JWH - Were you in the real estate business before Johnny got in?

Henry - I was in the mortgage and bonding business since the early '70's. Johnny got into the business right after W.T. Grant's shut down.

Bill - Yeah, I can tell you about that. Johnny had worked for Grant's until about 1974 when they closed down. Johnny, I believe, was the top salesman in the southeast, maybe the nation. He sold appliances. He said he would sell something, and then throw the appliance on a truck, and take it to them right then. During that time, I worked for Firestone, and I know what he is talking about. We did the same thing. We would tell them that if they bought the washer, we would deliver it right then. It was a benefit that Sears wasn't offering. So anyway, I'm sure he was one of the top salesman in the country. He's also a great athlete. He said one day this kid came into Grant's and stole something, and ran out the door. Johnny said he didn't know if he wanted to catch him or not, he just didn't want him to get away. Johnny took off running down Greensprings Highway. He said he just ran along behind him. The kid ran about 4 or 5 blocks, and then just stopped and sat down, all out of breath.

JWH - I know how he felt. I had PE classes with Johnny all through high school. In distance, even back then, he was in a class all by himself.

Bill - He used to come into work of a morning and say, "I ran down to Alabaster this morning." And he meant that literally. He ran to Alabaster. Anyway, getting back to what you asked. He started in real estate in late 1975. I was a broker at the time with a company called Realty Properties. A guy that worked there knew Johnny, and he suggested that Johnny come to work there. So he went to work in the brokerage division.

Johnny had long hair back then, he really had a shaggy look. When he first started selling real estate he had this old red Toyota pick-up truck. The thing was rusty and ragged. The first year he sold over a million dollars worth of real estate in that pick-up. We hauled people around in it, that truck was legendary. That's just a tribute to his personality, because people wanted to do business with him. He worked there for awhile, until about the middle of 1978. That's when the three of us became partners with Oxford Realty.

JWH - Johnny came from Grant's as a super salesman. Did that carry over to real estate?

Bill - When I left Realty Properties and started my own business, I really didn't know who he was. I mean he worked there, but I never paid any attention to him. I judged him by his hair, I guess. I took one look at him and I thought he would never make it. When they closed that place down one of the brokers said to me, "Don't let anything happen to Johnny, he'll carry you." Johnny started off as a cracker jack salesman. He knew how to close. Johnny has been in the Million Dollar Club every year since he's been in the business. He has been in the Club of Excellence, and he's gotten the Vulcan Award, which is 10 straight years over a million in sales. He even got it back in '79 and '80 when there were very few left in the business. The biggest company in town had only 12 agents in 1980. Interest rates were at 16%, and times were tough. You had to be really sharp to have made it in those days. Back then we didn't owe anybody, so Johnny and I would play golf everyday. We would be heading to Highland Golf Course by 9:00 a.m. We had some good times doing that. It seems we did fine. Life was simpler then.

JWH - Well, you guys outlasted the golf course.

Bill - That's right. We even made it through some of the things that happened on that golf course. One day we were at the course, and we might have had a beer or two. Johnny was driving the golf cart, and we were just flying down this hill. Well, Johnny's hat blew off. Johnny grabbed for his hat, and when he did, he turned the wheel, and the golf cart turned over. I ended up under the golf cart, and the battery acid started running out all over me. Johnny had to drag that cart off of me. I wasn't hurt bad. We had a lot of fun on that golf course.

JWH - Do you get to play golf now?

Bill - I haven't played in years. I bet I haven't played but maybe one time in 10 years, and Johnny doesn't play anymore, either. Let me tell you, when he did play, he could hit a golf ball. If he had played more, Johnny could have played with anyone. He could drive, he could chip, and he could putt. He's just one of those guys that can do anything. Don't you think so, Henry?

Henry - Yeah, no matter what sport you name, even if he had never played, he could pick it up and beat you at it.

Bill - That's right, he really is a tremendous athlete. Back in 1980 Van McAllister started working with us. We used to sit here sometimes 4 or 5 hours without a call. We get over 8,000 calls a month now. Anyway, we had this office putting cup, and we all had our putters here at the office. We would get back 30 to 35 feet from the cup, and see who could get the closest. Johnny would always beat everyone, he was darn good. Van came in for his first day wearing a business suit, carrying a briefcase, and we were all wearing tennis shoes, Bermuda shorts, and tee shirts, putting for a dollar a shot. McAllister took one look and knew he had found a home. I think that was the last time I ever saw him in a suit. He sells real estate down in Gulf Shores now.

JWH - Henry, tell me some stories about Johnny.

Henry - I remember one time when we hadn't been in business very long, and we had a management meeting at Bill's house down on the gulf. The first night there we went out to eat, just the three of us. We had this wonderful meal, a huge meal, and we left the restaurant so stuffed we could hardly move. On the way back to the house, Johnny asked if we could stop at the 7-11. He said he had to have something to eat. He went in and bought a case of Twinkees. He ate almost all of them before we even got back to the beach house. So, in addition to being a wonderful athlete, he is also a world-class eater. I guess it's because he burns so much energy. I have never seen anyone eat the way he can.

Bill - His eating is legendary.

JWH - What is it that is so appealing about Johnny?

Bill - He has a magnetic personality. Anytime he wants, he can be the center of attention because he is so outrageous and funny. He's got this Superman routine that he does where he gets behind a door and first you hear this sound of him flying through the air. Then you see his hands coming into the doorway, then his upper body. It's Superman flying, and it's one of the funniest things. He has lots of crazy antics like that. He is just a lot of fun.

Henry - Some say that Johnny is organized, but before you print that, you might want to look in his office, first. Sometimes it looks like a train wreck has happened in there. He is always busy, and always on the move. He just does not sit still for very long.

Bill - We used to go down to The Ox after work. We called it the Oxford Conference Room. If Johnny got there late, he would tell the bartender to give him three Bobby Allisons. That was what he called Miller Lite. He would down those three beers in a hurry to catch up. He has changed a lot. He got concerned about his drinking, and gave it up. He said he drank more than others knew. When he told me he had a drinking problem, I was surprised. I would never have thought that Johnny was an alcoholic. I was around him 50 hours a week or more. I guess I was around him more than his wife. I just never saw it, but it scared him and he quit, and that's what counts.

Meredith Montgomery
Daughter
Student

Meredith Montgomery

JWH - Meredith, tell me about your father.

Meredith - In 20 words or less?

JWH - Right, what's the first thing that comes to your mind?

Meredith - Crazy, funny, entertainer, loving, trainaholic, workaholic, looks great for his age, been through a lot in life, a great father.

JWH - Do you remember when he was still drinking?

Meredith - When he drank, it promoted a lot of his craziness. When you are under the influence of alcohol, you act differently. He really didn't need alcohol to be creative or funny or original. When he drank he had to be the life of the party, always. That's one of the characteristics of an alcoholic, I think. Back then, drinking came before family. I think it affected his work and his training, too. But alcohol is not in the picture anymore, which is wonderful. I think it's a shame that he got sober after my parent's divorce.

JWH - I get the sense that your parents get along quite well even after the divorce.

Meredith - They get along great. I have a lot of friends with divorced parents, and they are bickering all the time. But my parents have maintained their close and supportive relationship.

JWH - You work for your father, now, helping to keep him organized. As I have learned, Johnny is not too organized.

Meredith - He knows where everything is, he really is pretty organized. But there is something that always needs doing. There is always work here.

JWH - Are you going to follow in his footsteps as far as a real estate career is concerned?

Meredith - I was speaking to my mom earlier today about getting my real estate license. I would always have that to fall back on. Whether I want to or not, I will always be involved in real estate, because he and my mother have a number of properties. Someday, my sister and I will have to take over, so I need to know something about it. I will get my license sometime soon.

JWH - What other ambitions do you have?

Meredith - I like art, like my mom. I'd like to work as a curator for the museum, or something with art history.

JWH - What about music? Do you take after Johnny there?

Meredith - Oh, yeah, the music, there are so many sides to my father. I know he is talented, but I am not a performer, and I don't play any instrument. But my dad is a great guitar player, a great singer, and he can play the harmonica. His energy on stage is unreal, he was born to be in front of people. He was born to be on stage. Actually, he doesn't even need a stage. When I have friends come over, he can make them fall on the floor, he's so funny. They all say, "Your dad is so hilarious."

JWH - On the serious side, I can't conceive of what it takes to finish an Ironman competition.

Meredith - I can't either. I've been to four of them in Hawaii. Each one has it's own drama. The last time I went, he came home in an ambulance. It was awful. I wanted him to swear he would never do it again. Now, I don't know how I could ask him to do that. I worry that he just doesn't know his limits. I think he needs to remember that he has a family that cares about him. He is very healthy, but even healthy people can get into trouble. What's even worse, the next year he ran with a broken collarbone, and the doctors said he has a heart murmur. My sister and I both worry about him.

JWH - With his dedication, what have you learned from Johnny that you will carry with you all of your life?

Meredith - Mostly about God. He's taught me a lot about God. He has taught me that there is a time to be serious, and a time for fun. Everything that is important in life, he has taught me.

JWH - It is said that when a young lady is looking for a mate, that she is actually looking for a replacement for her father. The young man in your life is going to have some very big shoes to fill.

Meredith - I seem to look for tall guys, and that might be part of it. The last couple have been 6 footers, and my dad is 6'2". Sometimes I think that I don't want all the attention getting stuff, but then again, sometimes I do. I do look for characteristics like my dad. I never thought about that before, but I do.

Megan Montgomery
Daughter
Student

Megan Montgomery

JWH: Megan, how old are you?

Meg: Twelve.

JWH: Where do you go to school?

Meg: Our Lady of Sorrows School.

JWH: What grade are you in?

Meg: The seventh.

JWH: What's your best subject?

Meg: Science is the subject I do best, but I like math better.

JWH: Your father and I went to school together and we werent the best of students. Are you a good student?

Meg: I've made A-B honor roll all my life.

JWH: Your dad and I never made any honor roll. I'm sure your dad is very proud of you. When you think about your dad, what do you think about first?

Meg: He's just Dad. He's funny! He makes me laugh.

JWH: Do you ever tell people his jokes?

Meg: It's hard to because he can make a joke about anything. Sometimes it's not what he says but what he does.

JWH: Does he ever give you advice?

Meg: He tells me there are lots of people that are less fortunate than us, and not to be greedy. God has given us lots of things that we should be thankful for.

JWH: Do you ever go to church with your dad?

Meg: Sometimes

JWH: Lots of people say it's a miracle for your dad to be in church. So be proud when you do go to church with him.

Meg: I know.

JWH: Megan, what do you want the rest of the world to know about your dad?

Meg: That he is in the *Ironman* many times and he is really good at running, biking and swimming.

JWH: Do you ever go out and bike and run with him?

Meg: Yeah, sometimes I'll bike and he'll run. We go on these trails in Homewood. I go to a lot of his races and he will run the one-mile fun run with me. I've gotten lots of first places. Sometimes I go to the track with him on Tuesday nights and run with the track team and him.

JWH: Do you want to become a runner?

Meg: Maybe, I'm not sure.

JWH: What else would you like to tell the world about your dad?

Meg: He is the best dad in the whole world.

Bonnie Fuller
Receptionist
Oxford Realty

Bonnie Fuller

JWH - Johnny's life has touched a lot of people. I understand your son is one of those people. How did Johnny influence him?

Bonnie - My son is named Donald. He is 12 and he has asthma. His asthma has always prevented him from doing things that he would like to do. He has always looked up to Johnny and has been envious because he couldn't run like Johnny. We attended the Oxford Fun Run, but we came to walk it. That day I had all of my brothers and sisters there with me. The first thing I knew, I heard the shot of the starting pistol, and there went Donald running. That was a surprise, but I was even more surprised when Donald won the race. He ran that mile in 4 minutes and 57 seconds. He said he heard the gun, and he knew he had to race. He loves Johnny, and Johnny is a great influence on him. He talks about Johnny all the time; about all the races he has run, and medals he has won. Donald was so proud to be standing there that day with Johnny, holding that trophy. He was like Johnny that day, having the will to win. Johnny touches so many lives, and there are a lot of people like my son who love him.

Brian Dickens

Brian Dickens
Student

JWH - How do you know Johnny?

Brian - I met Johnny about 4 years ago. I ran track at Wallace State Junior College, and my previous coach, Stan Nawrewski, was a good friend of Johnny's. They went to school and ran track together at Livingston. Coach Nawrewski would send us to Birmingham for road races and additional training. Johnny is THE coach for distance runners in this part of the world.

JWH - So you know Johnny as a mentor?

Brian - Yes. He's that, and a whole lot more. He takes care of

me, and a whole lot of other people. He's my coach, my boss, and my support; he lets me stay here. He supports a lot of runners by finding them jobs, and making them stay in school. Things like that.

JWH - What are your aspirations as far as sports go?

Brian - I just want to run as well as I can in the time that's provided, and get my education, too. Basically, I want to do the best I can.

JWH - You have no aspirations to do the Ironman?

Brian - I don't know about all that. There's a lot of pain involved in doing the Ironman. I don't know if I'm ready for that.

JWH - What's your major?

Brian - Computer science. I have 2 years left to go. After that, I have a lot of things to decide.

JWH - Is there anything else you want to say about Johnny?

Brian - Like I said before, he helps me and a lot of others. Everyone that knows him knows what a great guy he is. He will do anything to help you in any way he can. He's a great athlete. We call him an Animal, which is a compliment. Anything you ever need, he offers it before you can even ask. I would describe Johnny as anything good that can be said about a person. I have never had anyone, outside of my family, help me like he has. I'd call him a true Christian.

Keith Knight
Corporate Administrator

Keith Knight

JWH - How long have you known Johnny?

Keith - I've known about Johnny for about 10 years. I met him about 1988, right after I started running. Every time I told someone that I had started running, they would ask me if I knew Johnny. I started hearing his name all the time. I used to train with a friend of mine, and we would see Johnny and his group at all the races. They would always beat us, and after a couple of years, we decided that maybe we should train with Johnny if we wanted to win. That's when I began training with Johnny and we became friends. I began to get into triathlons, and we spent a lot of time training together. Over the last couple of years our friendship has really grown.

JWH - When you switched to training with Johnny did your

running improve?

Keith - Yes it did. I started going to the track, and it was really interesting. We worked on intervals and did a lot of speed work and work on the track. The secret is the competition between a lot of runners with about the same speed. Training with them became competitions in themselves. I think that helped me more than anything, and Johnny was always there. He rarely misses a Tuesday night at the track. He's always there helping runners to improve themselves.

JWH - Everyone seems to have a Johnny Montgomery story. What's yours?

Keith - Beating Johnny was one of my goals in racing early on. I figured if I could ever beat Johnny, I would really have accomplished something major in racing. I remember the first time I beat him, too, at the Vulcan Run one year. I caught him with about 100 yards to go, passed him, and I will never forget it.

Just a few weeks ago we went over to Philadelphia, Mississippi for a triathlon. Wherever Johnny goes, he takes a big roll of duct tape. For whatever purpose, Johnny can fix any problem with duct tape. We were getting ready that morning, and Johnny pulled out that roll of duct tape. He said that he had lost the strap for his water bottle, and he was going to tape his water bottle to his bike, so he pulled off some tape and did that. Then he said that he needed to tape his power gel to the bike so he would have it to eat during the race. Well, he didn't stop there, he thought of three or four other things he needed that duct tape for, and by the time he was done he had used about half that roll of tape on his bike. The bike is supposed to be light and aerodynamic, but with all the tape, his bike probably weighed a couple of pounds more. But that's Johnny, he couldn't operate without his duct tape.

There for awhile, after we had our workouts on Tuesday nights, we would go to Johnny's house for pizza. We would order pizza and then get in Johnny's hot tub. We left a note on the front door for the pizza delivery person to come around the to the back door. This delivery guy came around the back, and sees Johnny and me kicked back in the hot tub with the bubbles going, so he didn't know if we were naked or not. He was sure nervous because he didn't know what was going on. He laid down the pizza, got his money, and left in a real big hurry. My wife loves that story.

JWH - I see a lot of trophies. Was Johnny an influence in winning them?

Keith - He definitely helped me a lot. I won my first triathlon trophy over in Philadelphia, Mississippi, and Johnny is undoubtedly the reason I am getting better. There is no truth in the idea that when you get older you can't get faster.

JWH - Has Johnny changed your diet?

Keith - I've been through many diet fazes, doing what you are supposed to do, and not supposed to do. For awhile there, I ate almost all carbohydrates, stayed away from fats and proteins. Then when I started training with Johnny, we would be in a 50 or 60 mile bike race, and at about mile 40, Johnny would say, "I can almost taste those hot-dogs down at Dino's." He would start talking about food, and when we got through with the race we would head over to Dino's in Homewood. The first time I went in there with him he walked up to the counter and ordered 4 chili-dogs and a cheeseburger. I thought he had ordered for both of us, but he turned to me and asked, "Keith, what do you want?" So I ordered the same thing, and we walked out of there with 8 chili-dogs and 2 cheeseburgers and went down to the Track Shak running store and ate every bit of it.

JWH - Let's talk about Johnny outside of athletics.

Keith - Johnny has always done a lot of things for a lot of people; most of those things nobody knows about. Besides spending a lot of time at the track, which I'm not sure everyone can appreciate all that means, there are lots of kids like Brian who he keeps busy. He does things for people without expecting any recognition or anything in return, getting them jobs and other things like that. When I meet people, and they know Johnny, the first thing they say is, "He's a great runner." Then they say, "He's one of the nicest guys I've ever met."

He has always been a great friend to me. Even more so in the last couple of years. He was going through some rough times about a year ago, and we shared some things with each other and became really close. He genuinely cares what is going on in my life, beyond running and real estate.

Johnny became a Christian about a year ago, and I can see a big difference in him. He doesn't let things bother him as much, and he realizes that things can affect you that you don't have any control over. He has an inner strength that he knows will see him through anything. He has said a lot of times that none of the stuff he has, the running, the house, business, whatever, none of that stuff is important. He says that when he dies, he knows where he is going, and that's what is important. Seeing Johnny change like that has made a big impression on me.

Terry Williams
Contractor

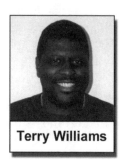

Terry Williams

JWH - How do you know Johnny?

Terry - I met Johnny about 5 years ago when I was cutting the grass in front of this here office we're in. He pulled up and introduced himself to me. He asked me if I would cut another yard for him. I've been friends and worked for him ever since.

JWH - Do you run?

Terry - No, I don't run. I just do a lot of work on Johnny's rental properties.

JWH - What do you want to say about Johnny?

Terry - I want to say that Johnny Montgomery is a special man. To me he's been an inspiration. He has taught me about achieving goals, and inspired me to reach my goals. Now I paint houses; I do interior and exterior work, and I got people that work for me. That's something that Johnny told me was going to happen, and I didn't believe him. He's a good friend, and a very special person. I respect him, and admire him a lot. He's an all around good guy.

JWH - What did Johnny tell you that changed your life?

Terry - He told me that he had done the same work that I was doing, and that there was nothing wrong with making honest money by hard work. But he told me that there were bigger things in store for me. At that time I didn't realize what he was saying, until it started happening.

He's a good Christian man. I went to see him when he got baptized. I wanted to make it a point to be there because he is special to me and to my family. I care a lot about him, and he's my friend. When my mama died 2 years ago Johnny was the only white man there in Church. He sat in the front row because he came just for me.

Barry McCully
Mayor
Homewood, Alabama

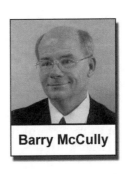

Barry McCully

JWH - How long have you been mayor of Homewood?

Barry - About 3 years now

JWH - What did you do before that?

Barry - I was on the City Council 8 years prior to that.

JWH - How did you meet Johnny?

Barry - Homewood is a very small community in the middle of a large metropolitan area. Anyone that is very active in the community will cross paths sooner or later, and as active as Johnny is, our paths have crossed a number of times.

JWH - You honored Johnny recently, didn't you?

Barry - I made a proclamation that declared a Johnny Montgomery Day here in Homewood. It was as a result of his unprecedented performances at the Ironman competitions. I'd have to go back in our records to give you an exact date, but it was last year. We were very fortunate to announce this honor at the City Council meeting where from time to time we recognize citizenship award winners from our middle schools. We felt like it was the perfect opportunity to tell the young people what Johnny has accomplished, not only in his participation in these events over the years, but in that particular year he had overcome injuries sustained during training. The obstacles he overcame just to participate were just short of unbelievable. I was able to point this out to this group of kids who were there representing their schools as citizenship award winners, and I hope this was an inspiration to them. It points out that we can all do a great deal more than we think we can, if we have the right attitude and persevere, as Johnny has.

JWH - What about Johnny as a real estate agent?

Barry - In the business world you do as much business on relationships as you do anything else. Johnny's company has a great reputation and good strong relationships within the community. I think they do quite well.

I think from the point of view of personal discipline and goal setting, Johnny should be held up to our young people as an example to live by and to try to emulate. What he has accomplished, and what he will accomplish takes a lot of discipline, and he has the character to overcome obstacles. He has those qualities that we would like to instill in our children, if we only knew how. We work at it as parents, as members of a community, but telling someone, "This is what you ought to do, and this is how you ought to behave," is not nearly as effective as showing them. Johnny has shown; and I'm sure he will continue to show them how to build character, how to be committed, and how to exercise personal discipline in one's life to accomplish worthy goals.

Martha Ann Cooper
Real Estate Sales

Martha Ann Cooper

JWH - Tell me about Johnny Montgomery.

Martha - First of all, I want to tell you he is my best male friend. I was raised by my father and he was an alcoholic, which really affected my life in a lot of different ways. Because of this, I attend meetings for the families and friends of alcoholics, and that's where I met Johnny.

I have learned that I can trust Johnny with anything, with my kids, my billfold, all my earthly possessions. You can't say that about too many people in this world. Trust is important; when you trust someone, then you can be their friend. Johnny and I can call each other up and say, "Come on over and let's watch TV." and we know that we can have an enjoyable evening just watching TV with a buddy.

It's true confession time now. Do you know what our favorite thing to do is? (laughter) We rub each other's feet! For a runner to have their feet rubbed is heavenly. The first time I rubbed his feet, I remember him saying, "You don't know...you don't know...how good that feels."

When he's been training, his muscles burn. He'll call me up and tell me, "I biked 76 miles today." I'll say, "What! You did WHAT!" He'll tell me, "Yeah, I just did 76 miles and I'm headed for the hot tub." If he doesn't work his muscles after a workout he won't be able to go the next day. It's a serious thing for an athlete like him, whereas with everybody else it's just to feel good. With Johnny it's mandatory, his training works his muscles hard, and the water is a big help.

JWH - Do you have any other true confessions?

Martha - Johnny cooks the world's best steak. He can cook a steak like no one else I know. I don't even like steak that much, because it's usually tough, but the way he does it, you barely have to chew it.

JWH - Tell us something most people wouldn't know about Johnny.

Martha - He is always busy! Between his running, swimming, biking, his job, and his children, there's no time left. I spend a lot of time at work, and I have two kids at home. Of course, my exercise is like a warm-up to Johnny. I don't see how he does it.

JWH - I hear a lot about his eating habits. What are your

observations?

Martha - First off, most athletes can't sit down and eat a huge meal. They have to eat these small meals all day long, continuously fueling their body. Johnny gets so hungry that he almost passes out at times, and he talks a lot about how hungry he is. He'll say, "When I get through, I'm going to Dino's, or Sam's, and I'm going to eat everything." or the Anchorage or wherever, and eat this, that, and the other. But it's all talk. He sits down and when he's full, that's it. He really doesn't eat that much at a sitting. He does have a lot of meals throughout the day, which is healthier. Or so I'm told. When he comes back from working out, he has a protein shake. He has different concoctions that he takes to keep his body going at the rate he demands from it.

JWH - Since you have been in real estate for 22 years , let's talk about Johnny's business.

Martha - He's got a lot of common sense. We are all blessed with different gifts, and one of Johnny's gifts is knowing what must be done to a house in order for it to sell. He will go into a house and he'll say, "We need to take those drapes down, paint this, and spruce up the front with some flowers." He will be right on target, knowing exactly how to dress it up to sell.

Johnny has a very positive outlook. We were talking the other night, and he said, "You know, it was right after Christmas that I started walking, and having a hard time doing that." And now just 9 months have gone by, and he's training for the Ironman in Hawaii. That's incredible to me. He is definitely in touch with his Higher Power. It's also very important to Johnny to be a good father. I think he's doing a good job at that, he really tries hard. Johnny is not a fake person. He will tell you up front exactly what he's thinking and feeling, and I like that. He is always upbeat and happy.

JWH - He's always been that way. Back in high school you either loved Johnny or you shied away from him. Positive emotions are contagious, and some people don't want positive emotions. A lot of people would sit back and watch.

Martha - I'll tell you something that's kind of personal. I have had to think about this. I don't mind being in the background, or even being a wallflower, but I have to think about it in terms of our relationship because Johnny commands attention. He doesn't do it consciously, but if Johnny is in a room eventually he will be the center of attention.

I was planning a party for all the people I have sold houses to. I thought about how neat it would be to have Johnny there, but the more I thought about it, the more I came to the decision that this was a party for my clients and me to be together. If Johnny came it would end up being Johnny's party, and I would fade into the background. That's not being malicious or mean. It was my party and Johnny understood.

Johnny is a funny person, and sometimes he can be so silly. Yesterday we were talking about one of his clients that is moving to Wing, Alabama. He said, "Can you say wing three times fast?" I said, "Of course, wing, wing, wing." Then he said, "Hellwoe!" like Elmer Fudd. Johnny can be so silly.

JWH - Do you think that Johnny is happy?

Martha - I think that happiness is within one's self. Johnny knows that he can be happy without someone else, and that God is at work whether he wins or loses in everyday life, or has a relationship. It's not that Johnny will not be disappointed if he loses, we've talked about this a lot of times. We want certain things to happen, but there is a lesson to be learned even when things don't go the way we want them to, and it is some preparation for something greater. We both believe this is true, and we both believe in a loving God.

JWH - This book will reach a lot of people. What would you like those people to know about Johnny?

Martha - I would want them to know that they can do anything. What I mean by that is that it doesn't matter who your mother was. It doesn't matter that your father drank all his life, or that he drank himself to death. It doesn't matter if you did or didn't have a great education. It doesn't matter if you didn't have the ideal marriage, or whether you had great kids or no kids at all. There are no excuses for not trying. You can achieve your dreams if you cut out all the excuses. God has a plan for us, and Johnny is working God's plan for him. He is very thankful to his God for all his blessings. I would like my son to learn this from Johnny.

Alan Perlis
Real Estate Sales

Alan Perlis

JWH - Alan, you're an author so you know what we are trying to do. How long have you known Johnny?

Alan - I guess I've known him for about 11 or 12 years. I had known him through the real estate business, but I didn't join Oxford Realty until 17 months ago. Johnny was instrumental in my coming to work here. I had co-oped a few deals with him, and I always liked Johnny a lot. He and Bill Waldrip always wanted me to come to work with them, so finally I did.

JWH - What happened to finally convince you to come to work with them?

Alan - Part of the reason was monetary, and part of it was because my old company was merging with another large company that was massive, with over 1,000 real estate agents. I'm just not that corporate. I like the way Johnny and these guys do business. They are really clear and up-front about things. I like working and being around Johnny and the rest of these guys.

JWH - Has Johnny got you running yet?

Alan - I run, but not at Johnny's level. I do about 4 or 5 miles just about every morning.

JWH - Not many are at Johnny's level.

Alan - There are very few, if any. I don't run competitively like Johnny does.

JWH - What would you like to say about Johnny?

Alan - He is who you see and meet. I mean he's open, available, and friendly. Johnny is honest, he is warm-hearted, and he's a fundamentally decent human being. What impresses me most about Johnny is he's just an easy-going guy who has become comfortable with himself. That took a lot of work, because I know his background. I knew he had an alcohol prob-

Johnny Montgomery

"Ironman"

8 Time
Ironman
Finisher

Kona,
Hawaii

BROOKS

Oxford
REALTY COMPANY
BIRMINGHAM, AL

Photo courtesy of Larry Arnold

"The Running Realtor"

lem, but I didn't know him well enough when he was fighting it to even know he was. I just knew him as a phenomenally gifted athlete and a great real estate agent. But I have learned more about what he's had to overcome, and how well he has done it. He is also a great father to his children, which I respect, being the father of five myself.

Another thing that can't be missed is Johnny's great sense of humor. He doesn't meet anyone who doesn't become a friend right away, and the way he ingratiates himself to people is through his humor. He's a very, very funny guy.

JWH - What else would you like to say about Johnny?

Alan - I want to talk about his dedication to everything he does, which is another thing that I admire about Johnny. He doesn't do anything half-assed, it's either all the way or he doesn't do it. That's not only true of his running, it's there with his commitment to his kids and to his work. I've never seen anyone with the well-spring of energy that he has, the dedication that he has toward whatever he is doing. There is nothing sloppy about him, even in terms of his appearance. This is a guy who came from alcoholic parents who probably didn't give him much of a childhood, who somehow found the way to find the best in himself. And he still works hard at it everyday. I almost think his running symbolizes the way he grabs hold of life and does his best with the material he's got. I don't mean just his body, but his mind, too. It's in the way he presents himself to people, a way in which he is incredibly polished. That seems ironic; because he is a country boy who talks like he had very little education. In actuality, he's bright and sophisticated, and a lot of that comes from working damn hard at developing himself.

JWH - What do you see in the future for Johnny?

Alan - I see more of the same. I really think he enjoys doing what he's doing now.

JWH - Alan, what's the title of your book?

Alan - "The Unofficial Guide to Buying a Home." The next one is going to be "The Unofficial Guide to Selling Your Home."

Scott Strand

Scott Strand
Manager
The Trak Shak

JWH - How long have you known Johnny?

Scott - I've known Johnny since I was 12 years old, when I started road racing. Before that I wasn't into running. I was a soccer player. Johnny was part of a group known as the Viaduct Vultures, made up of the best road racers around here. They would meet up at the old Shades Valley High School and do workouts on the track. After the workout they would sit under the viaduct where 280 crosses over, and have a few beers and tell tall tales. I would work out with them about once a week, so I've known Johnny a long time. He was one of the top overall runners back then. He hadn't started biking or swimming yet at that time. I remember when I first started I was always behind him, and then at some point along the way I caught him. By the time I went to college I had passed him.

JWH - I'm sure Johnny did the same in someone else's life.

Scott - You're right, and the same thing will happen to me, too.

JWH - You've won a lot and a lot of people look up to you. Tell us about yourself.

Scott - I walked on at Auburn University. I had a hard time getting scholarship money, but I ended up making All-American, and was SEC Champ in the steeplechase. When I got out of school I didn't want to stop running. A lot of times when you get out of school, it's a real struggle because you don't have that team support or the coaching behind you. I struggled for about three years, then in '94 I qualified for the Nationals. I made the finals for the Steeplechase for the last five years. In '96 I was a finalist and finished 6th in the Olympic finals. The best thing I've done is made the National Team and traveled with them.

JWH - Was Johnny an influence along the way?

Scott - He was early on. When I was in high school he was always there encouraging me, trying to get me to do the right thing. He was definitely a big influence early on. As I've gotten older I've formed my own ideas about what I need to do, but he's still always there. He'll come by and encourage me, getting a good word in. Now we kind of do that in a mutual way, encouraging each other.

JWH - How did you feel the first time you beat Johnny?

Scott - I really can't remember exactly when that was. I probably felt better than he did. (laughter) I do remember that he

College Graduation

found an old picture of us running at the Montclair Run. I was about 15 or 16 then. He said he beat me that day, but it had to be around then that I beat him for the first time. Running is a competitive life, and when you win you don't hold it over people's heads. You don't know who will win the next race.

JWH - From what I hear, you two have been pretty competitive for a long time. Putting that aside, what would you like to say about Johnny?

Scott - I want to say that Johnny is one of the most motivated people that I've ever been around. No matter what he does, he wants to do it well. I don't think I've ever seen him down, or in a bad mood. He's always upbeat and positive, he's just a pleasure to be around. He always has a great attitude.

JWH - How does he look for winning his age group in the Ironman next month?

Scott - I know that he's competitive in his age group, and I wouldn't bet against him. I do know that this year he seems to have worked out a lot harder than in years past. After he got qualified he's been really motivated. He's doing more training and longer rides than I've ever known him to do, and I think he'll be ready. Like I said, I wouldn't bet against him.

Milton Bresler
Sales Representative

Milton Bresler

JWH - Let's talk about Johnny Montgomery

Milton - I've known Johnny ever since Moby Dick was a minnow. We knew each other from track and field back in high school together in the '60's. We didn't go to the same school. I went to a small private school called Birmingham University School which is now part of Altamont School up on Red Mountain. I knew who he was, though, and he knew who I was, because we competed against each other in athletic events. We really didn't get acquainted until he went to Livingston University, and I went to Auburn. I had a lot of respect for him because of his athletic abilities in track. Luckily for me, he was a couple of years older than me, so I didn't have to compete every event against him. There were only a couple of events that we competed in with each other. I didn't really get to know him well until he moved to Birmingham and started working for Grants. I never had to really compete against Johnny until I got into road racing.

JWH - Milton, we want you to tell us the secret of what it took to be a Viaduct Vulture.

Milton - To be one of the Vultures you had to meet every Tuesday afternoon at Shades Valley High School to do interval training. Depending on how you finished the workout would determine who would have to buy the cooler of beer next week. After the workout we would always go up under the Red Mountain Expressway, and sit there and drink beer. After the workout we would get trashed. One of the guys made a T-shirt that had Viaduct Vultures with a vulture sitting on the side of the Expressway with beer cans all around him. I still have my T-shirt. I was one of the founding members.

JWH - When did you get into road racing?

Milton - In Birmingham, road racing started getting really popular back in the '70's when they started the Vulcan Run. That was around '76 or '77. Since then we've had a lot of fun. There were times when we were very, very competitive. He and I would even compete in the workouts we did with each other. We were great motivators for each other, because we both had a competitive spirit. One of the things that I greatly admire about Johnny is his competitive nature. I think we have a mutual respect for each other, over and above the competition, and we were able to maintain a very good friendship and a strong bond.

JWH - Then you knew Johnny during his drinking years?

Milton - I never knew at the time that Johnny had a drinking problem. He has since shared that with me, when I was dealing with my own drinking problems. Of course, I was oblivious at the time because I was dealing with my own share of problems. I went my way and he went his way and we would meet on our common ground, which was running. That's what held us together, both as individuals, and our friendship during that time, was running.

We were very competitive during those early years. I couldn't tell you if he beat me more times then I beat him. We were not always competing in the same age group. He was just enough older than me that sometimes we were and sometimes we weren't. Over the last 10 years Johnny's running has blossomed into world class, and I'm still only competitive locally.

JWH - How will he do at the Ironman This year?

Milton - This is his 8th Ironman. Unfortunately, Johnny has not performed well in the first six. It was an injury related problem sometimes. And once I remember he competed right after being sick. He has struggled during those six competitions, but he finished every one of them. I really hope this is his year. From what I have seen the last few months of his workouts, he's ready to do well this time. I look forward to tracking his progress this year over the Internet. He has been on TV here, and a lot of people think that this will be Johnny's year.

JWH - What would you like to tell people about Johnny?

Milton - This book you are writing is going to be an inspirational story. I think Johnny has a unique story to tell, with the adversity that he has overcome. To me, his life story would make a great movie. I love to hear the stories about running with the moonshine to protect his father, and about his growing up the way he did down in Tuscaloosa County. I love his stories about selling refrigerators at Grants. That's what really got him in the business of selling. Johnny has had a commitment to overcome all kinds of obstacles to make something of himself. He did it not to please others, but for himself. His story is one that we can all get strength from.

I value our relationship and I think we share a special bond. I can go for weeks, months, or even years without seeing or hearing from Johnny, and when we meet again, it is like nothing is changed in our friendship. There are very few real friends in a lifetime, and Johnny is one of those few to me. A true friend is not someone that tells you how to run your life, but is there to support and understand you, and offers advice only when asked. We learn from that and draw strength from it.

The bottom line to all this is doing something you are proud of. I grew up in a family with alcoholism, also. I had to overcome some of the same things that Johnny did, but it certainly made me a stronger person. I can relate to Johnny because we both shared some of the same struggles, and he has always been very supportive of me. He has always built my image up in the running community, even when we were most competitive. Johnny doesn't have a mean bone in his body. He's very kind to everyone, and always sees the best in everyone. That's why people want to be around him, he has a kind heart.

The strength I get from Johnny is to overcome obstacles. I'm on my third surgery, and I want to make a comeback with my running. I still haven't achieved my personal goals in running. I will never be in the class that Johnny is in, but the personal gratification is very rewarding to me. Of all our running community, Johnny has been the most resilient. When I was in the hospital a couple of weeks ago he came to visit me. He told me he swims 5,000 meters a day in the pool at 5:30 in the morning. Remember that Johnny used to be as skinny as that light post there. He had no upper body strength whatsoever. Eight or nine years ago, when he got into triathlons, he was as scared of the water as a two year old, but he learned how to swim. I just admire that. When you decide to do triathlons, you are looking at a five to seven hour a day commitment to training. Johnny just has a great deal of commitment.

John Petelos, M.D.
Pediatrician

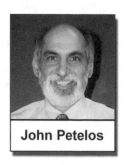

John Petelos

JWH – John, you also are a runner, aren't you ?

John – Yes. I ran at Ensley High School in both track and cross-country. I quit running during my twenties. I was in medical school, plus I had taken up some bad habits, like smoking. Then I started running again when I was 29, doing marathons. After I qualified for, and ran in , the Boston Marathon, I decided I wanted to do triathlons. I started doing triathlons in '83 and qualified for my first Ironman in 1986.

JWH – How many Ironman Competitions have you been in?

John – I've done two. I qualified another time, but didn't go.

JWH – How long have you known Johnny?

John – I was living in Panama City (FL) when I got back into running. I came up here to do the Vulcan Run a few times while I was living in Florida. I saw Johnny and knew who he was, but he didn't know who I was. When I moved to Birmingham in 1989 I met Johnny, and by that time he knew who I was because I had sponsored the Gulf Coast Triathlon, which he had participated in. I can even remember the day I met Johnny, because I had just joined the Y. It was the first time I had gone there to use the Y's facilities, and it was early in the morning. It was my first really long run since moving back to Birmingham. Johnny was there and we began talking. We ran together that morning and we have been friends ever since.

JWH – Can you remember the first time you beat Johnny?

John – I got to be a strong runner about the time I turned 40. I was really running well then, and I could actually beat Johnny except in the short races. He won those and the triathlons, which I was running back then. I can't say I ever remember Johnny beating me. (laughter) We were in different age groups too, but I would race against him. I can't remember the times I beat Johnny, but I sure can remember the times he beat me. (laughter)

JWH – What do you want to tell the world about Johnny?

John – He has a great sense of humor. He is a real country boy and has such a way of describing things. I get tickled just listening to him, he has such a colorful way of speaking. I really enjoy being around him.

The thing about Johnny is he is such a positive person. There would be times when I was down and out, like if I had a bad race, and Johnny would always come up to me and try to build me back up. He would give me confidence. He made me believe in myself. He has the ability to re-motivate you.

JWH - Tell me a Johnny Montgomery story.

John - We did the Powerman Duathlon out in Irondale. I never will forget it. I was trying to make a comeback running and biking, but I had not been training the way I should have. I

thought I was ready, but I wasn't. Johnny tells the story this way. He says when he went around me on the bike he looked back into my eyes and knew from the look that he had me whipped. He says he knew I was a goner. He knew I wasn't going to be a threat that day. You also need to know this, for two weeks every year we're in he same age group.

Let me tell you something else. I'm a real stickler with language usage and grammar. When I met Johnny the first thing that made an impression on me was the way he used improper grammar. One day Johnny and I were talking with Jerry Fitzgerald, who is a respiratory therapist from Mississippi, and a country boy himself. Johnny was talking and said something that was grammatically incorrect. When I tried to correct him, Fitzgerald looked at me and said, "John, there is no way. It's just his way of talking at this point in his life it's not going to affect him. He's just not going to change anything!" I realized what he said was the truth, so I no longer tried to correct Johnny's use of the English language.

Johnny is the master of efficiency, and I've learned a lot from him in this area. How to put things in a certain place, how to set things up to cut down on wasted time during transitions between the swim and the bike, or the bike to the run. I think Johnny was the first one to come up with using elastic. Rather than pinning his number to his shirt, he used the elastic from his underwear. I knew it was from his underwear because you could read 'Fruit of the Loom' all around it. Later on they started selling this same idea, but Johnny still uses his own homemade version.

Linda Baker
Waitress
Anchorage Restaurant

Linda Baker

JWH - How long have you been a waitress here at the Anchorage?

Linda - I have been here 17 years, and Johnny has been a customer for all of those 17 years. Out of all the runners who have come in here, he's the only one that has stuck with me. All the rest disappeared, but Johnny stayed. He's been coming here so long that I know his credit card number by heart, and we don't even talk about the tip. I know how much it is and I put it on the card myself.

JWH - What would you say is Johnny's favorite food?

Linda - In the morning time I would say grits; he loves grits. He usually gets scrambled eggs with grits, bacon and toast. And he wants extra grits. It's a must on the extra grits. Lunch time, he likes okra. Tuesdays he likes the dressing but leave off the gravy. He likes the macaroni , and sometimes he likes black-eyed peas. It depends on whether he wants to eat a lot, or he is eating light.

JWH - What, no meat?

Linda - Johnny very seldom eats meat. He may eat bacon at breakfast time, but lunch time he sticks with the vegetables. Yep, Johnny eats vegetables mostly.

JWH - Some people have told me about how much he eats. What's the truth about how much he eats?

Linda - He finishes everything on his plate. He's big on bread, and he can really slop down them rolls. He went somewhere and came back hooked on Louisiana Hot Sauce, which he never asked for until sometime in the last year. I don't know where he got on the sauce. I don't know where he went. He never takes me anyplace; but he always comes to see me. (laughter)

JWH - What do you want folks to know about Johnny?

Linda - He is one of the best guys I know. He's a very, very good person, and a good customer. He's Honest and funny. He's just Johnny, you know, everybody around here loves him.

Gary Fenton
Pastor
Dawson Memorial Baptist Church

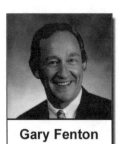

Gary Fenton

JWH - Tell me about Johnny.

Gary - I've gotten to know Johnny through the church. The first time I met him, it was at a restaurant with a friend. We were at New York Pizza and got to visiting. We sort of struck up a friendship there that day, and then he started visiting our church. I was really amazed at the determination of a guy his age who would stay in the kind of shape that he does. He and I talked about his overcoming some of his past difficulties, and I was struck by how deeply committed he was to doing this. He became very interested in the Christian faith, but the thing that impressed me the most was he was not looking for easy answers. He knew what he wanted to do and he wanted to be sure he was doing things the right way. In the New Testament Jesus tells us that you to count the cost. Johnny's not going to take his Christian faith lightly. Before he made his faith public he wanted to make sure that he was serious about it. It was a very touching thing when he joined our church because not all the people knew his story or his background. He had come a long way to be standing before our church and publicly acknowledging Jesus Christ as his personal Savior. It was also very special when he was baptized. It is so great to see someone work through that process, not wanting to take any shortcuts. We talked right in this room about whether he was ready for this step.

JWH - Johnny was saved right in this room, wasn't he?

Gary - Yes. I think in many ways Johnny knew Christ before he came to this room that day. He didn't quite know how to put it all together, but he had already accepted Christ. He knew what he needed to do, and what needed to happen. It was just sort of the formal moment here where he became a Christian.

I feel the decision was made before that day.

JWH - I have known Johnny just about all of my life. I know he has gone through a great change, and I feel he is being used by God in some powerful ways. Do you sense that?

Gary - I really do. Johnny is very honest about who he is. Most people are so afraid that someone will discover the truth about what they used to be. Then there are others that carry the past like a crown, almost as if they are proud of it, and they tend to glamorize it. Then there are those that carry it like the cross that it is. It is something that has been forgiven, and they are very open about it. They don't try to hide it, but it is not something that they brag about. I think with Johnny, he carries it like a cross in that if people want to know, he tells them. He doesn't make it look good, or glamorize it. As a result, it really helps troubled people to talk to him. He comes across as a guy who has been down the path and knows what he's talking about.

Johnny and I have an arrangement. There are some people he can help better than I can, because I haven't walked down all the roads that he has. I have studied and learned about these things, but if there is someone that needs help, I can give Johnny a call, or they can call him, and that is between them. They can tell me if they want to, but there are a lot of men who need another man to talk to instead of a preacher. They need someone who has personal experience, and will be honest with them. I think that is one way God uses Johnny, he uses his honesty and openness.

JWH - Do you want to say anything else about Johnny?

Gary - Johnny is a person who is really accessible. He is always moving fast, but he is never in a hurry, and there is a distinction. I've watched Johnny because he doesn't let any moss grow under his feet. He's moving all the time. But if someone needs to talk to him, he stops, even if it will make him late for an appointment. Some old legend said that hurry does not cause you to sin, it is a sin. I think that is because you are always passing things by when you are in a hurry. I have been amazed as I watch Johnny from a distance. This is something that we have never talked about, but even though he has a schedule, if you need to talk, he has time.

JWH - I know you have inspired him, but has he inspired you to start running?

Gary - Well, he's inspired me to start exercising, but not running. I do find it interesting that when I'm around him, I want to increase my exercise program. Johnny is inspirational. He really is. Johnny is a guy who lives with his heart and as a result, at times will be disappointed with himself. He sets such high goals for himself. Better to set goals too high and be disappointed, than to set them too low. I'm one of Johnny's biggest fans.

The day Johnny joined the church.

Bobbie Wright
Resort Management

Bobbie Wright

JWH - How do you know Johnny?

Bobbie - I know Johnny from my running days, from about 20 years ago. I think I started running in about 1978. The first time I heard about Johnny, he was having one of his famous beer-keg parties after a marathon.

JWH - What was Johnny like back then?

Bobbie - He was a lot like he is now, he was everybody's friend. He would do anything for anybody. But back then if you said Johnny Montgomery you would immediately think of beer drinking and partying. Johnny always had a keg at his house. He was the one who always had the parties at his house, he was the Pied Piper of the running group.

JWH - So you were around during the Viaduct Vulture days?

Bobbie - (laughter) I was; I was a member of the Viaduct Vultures. I should have been the first girl to get a tee-shirt, but I wasn't and it pissed me off. They gave these other girls their shirts, and even though I'm the original party girl and runner, I was the third girl to get a shirt. I was the girl who hung out with the guys; now I'm sure that is what my mother wants to read in a book. (laughter) I was the first girl to go out after Tuesday night workouts and drink with the guys for 5 or 6 hours.

JWH - How did that affect Wednesdays?

Bobbie - Wednesdays were not the funniest days. I would always plan Wednesdays so I would not have an early morning meeting. We did not plan anything on those days that we would have to think about. Johnny always said on Wednesdays you get that red dot disease. That's where you pull your head up off the desk and you have this red dot in the middle of your forehead. A lot of people got red dot disease on Wednesday mornings.

JWH - Johnny no longer drinks, has that changed him?

Bobbie - Yeah, Johnny's changed; first off, Johnny is one of a kind. There ain't ever going to be anyone else like him. When he was drinking he would sit and tell one joke right after another. Then after he first quit drinking he became a lot more serious and a lot quieter. Now he is more like his old self and can tell jokes and be funny without drinking.

Right after he and Susie separated he was really drinking heavy, he really worried me. Those were really tough times for Johnny. I took him home a few nights. Back then he was drinking way too much, so I'd hang out and make sure he got home okay. I was always there, and being a woman my nurturing side took over, I guess. The rest of the guys would get up and leave and there sat Johnny at the end of the bar barely able to keep his head up.

JWH - Can you remember any road trips with Johnny that were out of the ordinary?

Bobbie - We used to have a big master's track event, the Southeastern Championship, that was held in Atlanta. This was back in '80 or '81 and we would have 30 or so people go over there. Johnny could win at any and everything. He could run, he could do hurdles, he could throw the javelin, anything, any event, Johnny could do it. He would enter all these events and win gold medals one right after another. The thing about Johnny is he is so kind. I was never a fast runner, so I said to Johnny, "I've got to do hurdles but you have to be fast and you have to be super coordinated." Johnny would never say that I was too slow and clumsy to run hurdles, he would say, "We don't have anyone to throw the javelin, why don't you go and learn to do that?" He would put me over into the field events without hurting my feelings, and let me know that I could contribute. We won that 1980 championship by something like 200 points. And we partied that night, we were all sitting around the pool drinking beer and eating Johnny's favorite which is pork rinds and Tabasco sauce. There was this guy named John Grider there and he wanted to be a Viaduct Vulture real bad. So Johnny and the other guys told him that if he wanted to become a Vulture he had to learn to drink Tabasco sauce. Johnny took a big bottle of Tabasco sauce and put his finger over the opening and turned it up like he was drinking the sauce. Each of the other guys did the same thing, and when it was my turn I told them to pass me, I couldn't do it. The guy still hadn't caught on, so he took the bottle and drank it to prove himself. We kept on drinking and the bottle of Tabasco sauce kept getting passed as well. So this guy ended up drinking a whole bottle of Tabasco sauce, he really had no clue. The next day he was sick, I mean sick as a dog. He had paid his dues to become a Viaduct Vulture.

JWH - Is there a serious side to Johnny as well?

Bobbie - Johnny is a motivator; when you are down you can always call on Johnny, and he will lift you up. I'd say, "Johnny, I'm going through some bad times, can I talk to you?" He would talk me out of being depressed, letting me know that there are others out there that have it a whole lot worse than you do. He is always encouraging. Back when I first started thinking about doing triathlons, I asked him if he thought I could do it. He said, "Can you run?" I said, "Yeah," He said, "Can you swim?" I said, "Yeah," Then he said, "What's your question?" He helped me, I bet he has helped hundreds, if not thousands, of people.

Johnny is serious about being a good father, that's important to him. The running has helped him through a lot of things in life, and he has made a lot of friends through running, but he would rather be known as a good father than a good runner. I know that feeling has intensified since he became a Christian.

Eddie Elrod
Mortgage Broker

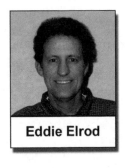

Eddie Elrod

JWH - Eddie, tell us about your running.

Eddie - I've been running since I was 30 years old, so I guess I was a late starter. I was always active, I played basketball during high school, but I started smoking right after that. I guess I just never cared about being healthy. When you're young you just don't think about your health, you take it for granted. One day, a friend of mine told me he had just run 5 miles. I said, "Run, I get tired driving 5 miles." The guy was Johnny Turner, a very good friend of mine. At that time he was a professor at Auburn; he had been the saxophone player in our band, The Swinging Playboys, back in the '60s. I got to talking to him and he told me how much better he felt since he had started running. About a week later I turned 30, and I got out an old pair of tennis shoes, which were actually basketball shoes, and that's what I wore running that first day. I ran 3 miles that day, stopping 4 or 5 times. Of course I was sore, and I didn't run for a week after that, but then I bought some real running shoes. I figured running was something you can do by yourself at a very low cost. You can run anytime you want to; midnight, 6 in the morning, rain or shine, it didn't matter. That's why I started running.

I met some other people who ran, and I did the Vulcan Run in 1979. A couple of years after that I met the running group here in Birmingham, which Johnny has always been involved in. That was in the days of the Viaduct Vultures.

JWH - Tell us about the Viaduct Vultures.

Eddie - I wasn't in the first incarnation of the Viaduct Vultures. I got involved a couple of years after that. When I got hooked up with them, it was a thing where new people coming on the track had to prove themselves. If you got out and won your age group in a race, or you did what we called show up and throw up, which was showing up at the track 3 times in a row, throwing up at least one of those times, you would probably get a t-shirt. It was a very big deal to receive a Viaduct Vultures shirt in those days. Everyone wanted one, but very few ever got one.

JWH - How does Johnny look for the Ironman this year?

Eddie - I think this year Johnny has a real good chance. He's in the best shape I've ever seen him in. For a guy 53 years old he's in incredible physical condition. He's competitive in his age-group nationally, if not worldwide. He's swimming better than I have ever seen him swim. He's always struggled with that in the past. For the last couple of years he has really been working on his swimming, working out with the Master's team a couple of days a week. He's got his stroke down, and he's doing some weight work. His running has always been there, because he's been running ever since he had to crawl under that barb wire back in Tuscaloosa. His biking has also improved. In all three events he's improved, and like I said, he's in the best shape I have ever seen him in. This year he has been to Switzerland, Canada, and I think Chicago. He's been in some really big races, and I think that will help him. It's easy for Johnny to go out and win any of these local races, not that they are easy. But for Johnny it's no big deal. It's a different ballgame going to a worldwide event where people are coming from everywhere trying to win. He's thrown in there with a lot of different guys in his age group who are as good as he is. Johnny is very, very competitive, and I think he has a good opportunity to place in his age group. That would be a phenomenal thing for him. We are all pulling for him to do it, and if he can get out of the water in the time frame that he has set for himself, and do it without getting leg cramps which he is prone to, he can place in his age group this year.

JWH - Let's go back and see if you can remember some experiences running with Johnny.

Eddie- -We went to Philadelphia, Mississippi year after year for their triathlon. It's called The Heart of Dixie Triathlon. We used to do this road trip every year.

   I remember Johnny and I going to a triathlon in Mobile a few years ago. That weekend we cried together, we got drunk together, and we laughed together. It was a very emotional weekend. We listened to sad country songs; we were both going through some tough times in our lives, and I remember sitting on the balcony down there, listening to George Jones and just sobbing, crying uncontrollably. The next day we got up, shook off the emotions, and ran the triathlon.

JWH - Do you think Johnny is a different person now that he's quit drinking?

Eddie - I don't think he's a different person, but his attitude is different. There may be a lot of folks that don't know Johnny well that might think he's drinking when he's not, because of his antics, his comic take on things. But that's just Johnny. I think what's different about Johnny these days is his attitude about life. Johnny is a very caring person, and he wants to help everyone with their problems. If Johnny is your friend, he is your friend all the way. I know his health is better now that he's not drinking. I love Johnny either way, but I do like him better since he quit drinking.

JWH - You are in the mortgage business, and Johnny is in the real estate business. Do you do business together?

Eddie - He sells houses and I finance houses. He sells them, and then he sends the clients to me. Johnny is the Running Realtor. Everybody in Birmingham knows Johnny for promoting running, as well as real estate in all his advertising and PR materials. He treats his business just like he treats running. He's is full-on. He has been at it a long time, and is really good in the business. I think he's a natural born salesman. I bet in grade school he was selling something. He sold for Grants, and he sold washing machines to people with no indoor plumbing. If he could do that, he could sell anything.

JWH - Eddie, there's a part of Johnny that you can give us insight into since you were a huge influence in Johnny's musical accomplishments.

Eddie - Johnny is the type of guy that can do almost anything. I don't know if Johnny is a bowler or not, but I guarantee if he went to the bowling alley, and you put a bowling ball in his hands, you'd have a hard time beating him. The same is true for throwing horseshoes, or anything else. And it is true for music. Johnny is not the best singer in the world, but he loves to give it a shot, and he's not shy about it. He found out that I sing and play the guitar on the way to a race one day, and he said he was interested in learning to play guitar. I told him I would bring my guitar over one night and we would just sit and strum. So we did that. He didn't have a guitar, so I brought an old one that I 'd had since high school. It was an old Werco that Johnny says he is going to return, but it's been 20 years now, so I have my doubts. It's a real old guitar with the action about a half an inch from the neck to the strings. That's what he learned on. We would get together and I would play some three chord songs. Johnny would say he wanted to learn a song, so I would write it down and the next time I would come over he would have the song down. We had some great times sitting around strumming, singing, and playing.

But Johnny is really self taught. I showed him a few chords, but he really learned on his own. Some other people showed him some things along the way, too.

Johnny called me not too long ago and said, "Eddie, you won't believe it, but I listened to this song and figured out the chords they're using. I did it by myself without any help from you or anyone else!" I said, "That's great, Johnny!" He's getting the knack of being able to hear different chords and finding the sound on his guitar. Before he could strum the guitar and now he can play the guitar. Back during some early real estate functions, I would back Johnny up on guitar. That's when he was doing his Elvis routine.

JWH - Eddie, when did you get into music?

Eddie - I sang my first solo in third grade. I sang 'Mockingbird Hill' at an annual PTA affair at school. I think I was picked because I was the only one in the class who could carry a tune, and I remember being scared to death. I always sang in church, beginning in the youth choir. In high school I got in the adult choir. I also sang in the boy's chorus in high school. Singing has just always been a part of my life. My mom started playing piano early in her life, but when we were growing up we couldn't afford a piano. The house was too small for one anyway. Mom also sang in the church choir.

In high school we formed a band that was finally known as the Swinging Playboys. For whatever reason, we went through three or four names. We played a lot of Battle of the Bands, and even recorded a couple of records while we were still in high school. We had a wonderful time playing rock 'n roll back then in the '60's. After high school the band started falling apart because everyone was going in different directions. I stayed in music, playing an acoustic single act in coffee houses, night clubs, and bars. After that I was in a duo for awhile, and then I sort of got out of music for about ten years. A few years back a friend of mine and I got together and formed the Boomin' Baby Boomers. We do '60's music, mixed with some original tunes. Right now we're working on a motion picture project. I've been involved with music all of my life.

JWH - You and Johnny are the Blues Brothers. What goes on backstage as well as on-stage?

Eddie - First of all we do the old Blues Brothers, Belushi and

Ackroyd. We're about the same size although Johnny is a little taller. We're both thinnish, so there's no Belushi visual image, and since Johnny is taller, I ended up being Belushi, or Jake. I have to put padding in my shirt to look like him. We started this about 12 or 13 years ago when there was a real estate function they wanted Johnny and me to do play during the band's break. We were at his house playing guitars one night and there was a commercial for the Blues Brother's movie, or Saturday Night Live, I forget which and that commercial sparked something. So we decided to do a Blues Brothers routine. We went down to the Salvation Army and bought each of us a cheap suit. We made a tape of 'Soul Man,' and we set the jambox up in the middle of the floor and came out swinging the handcuffs and the chain connected to the briefcase, and we were off. Everybody had a ball, they just loved it. We improved it by renting the video of the Blues Brothers movie, and picked up the exact steps and movements of Ackroyd and Belushi. By the way, Johnny is uncanny in the way he moves just like Ackroyd. Since then we have progressed, and made it part of the Boomin' Baby Boomers act. Johnnys' a great Blues Brother, and a great partner to have.

Back stage what happens is I usually run back there from having done a previous song with the band. When I get back there Johnny is usually outfitted with his sideburns on and his suit. He's pulling my socks off, and I'm stuffing pillows in my shirt, and it's all got to be done in about 45 seconds. The last thing we do is Johnny slaps my sideburns on for me. I don't know how we do it, but it gets done. It's hectic, but it's a helluva lot of fun.

JWH - Could Johnny have made it as an entertainer?

Eddie - Oh yes. I used to say that Johnny missed his calling, but I don't say that anymore. We all end up doing what we should do. I'm not saying that Johnny missed anything, but he could have definitely been a Steve Martin. Or, I could say that Steve Martin could have been a Johnny Montgomery. You could say it either way. Johnny is very, very talented in that area. Entertainment is a very broad word, and it can mean a lot of different things. Johnny is definitely an entertainer, and he could have gone on in that direction quite easily. He would have probably ended up in Hollywood; but whether that would have been good for him or not, only God knows. I used to say that he missed his calling, and a lot of people still say that. But I think he found his true calling, whether he missed something else or not.

JWH - Eddie, what would you like to tell the world about Johnny Montgomery?

Eddie - Johnny Montgomery is an absolutely fierce competitor in any and everything he does. He is a true and loyal friend and business associate-and I love him.

Michael Shane Spiller

Michael Shane Spiller, Ph.D.
Professor
University of Montevallo

JWH - You ran against Johnny several times. Tell me about Johnny.

Michael - Johnny and I have competed in a number of races. He's the type of person that sticks out because he's always got a group of people that follow behind him. He runs so well, and he's always so friendly at the races. He stuck out for me because we ran at about the same times. There was one year that we ran a race in Tuscaloosa. I ran a 17:19, and he ran a 17:17. He did just enough to stay just ahead of me the whole time, and he really watched me that last mile. If I sped up, he would speed up just enough to stay ahead of me. The next year we both ran the same race and neither of us had trained very well. Neither of us was doing too good a job. I ran about an 18:40, and he ran an 18:38. It was the exact same thing. He would stay just enough ahead of me to beat me; especially keeping me in his eye that last mile. He's that kind of competitor. He will pick someone out, and he's not going to let them beat him.

The other race that sticks out is the Midnight Run in Tuscaloosa, which he won. I can't remember exactly what year that was, but I was in the best shape I had ever been in. It was a small race but the people that were competing were all really good runners. George Brown came in second. He was the top runner in Tuscaloosa for several years. We had Mike Hamm who was a former Olympic qualifier. He was extremely good. There were no slouches in that race, and Johnny won. He just pulled away from us. I was in the lead for the first mile or so, then Johnny took over. It's not like I died or anything, but Johnny just buried me. I think I ran 17:01, and I was extremely proud of my time; until I got up the next morning and read the newspaper. There was this article about a 50 year old beating everyone else. I was probably 25 then; half his age. It didn't bother me too much because I knew the kind of training that Johnny did, and the kind of competitor he is. I'm personally happy to see him continue that way. It's the kind of thing that we try to emulate in the running community. We want to keep going to become that kind of runner later on. I talk to Johnny at every event, but we never got to the point of being really good friends. There was one year that he came down for the Wildcat Run at his high school. He makes that every year. I didn't run because I was finishing up my dissertation. Johnny came to me and said that he was surprised I wasn't running that day; that he missed me on the course. We're not the best of friends because we don't live in the same community. When I moved to Montevallo, all the realtors knew him, and they all knew what he did. Seems they all knew some little myth about Johnny and his running. This seems to be pervasive throughout the Birmingham community. I started talking to some of the runners here, and getting involved in the running community. They would always compare everything to the Oxford Realty Club. I knew exactly who they were talking about. I could start naming off names. They were amazed that they had that kind of notoriety. I think Johnny is very well known in this state. People know his name right off the bat. I have always kept up with what he is doing. I recently picked up my running again, and the first thing I want to do is get out there and beat him. That would be a big accomplishment despite his age.

Stan Arthur
Convenience Store Owner

Stan Arthur

JWH - Stan, when I say Johnny Montgomery what comes to mind?

Stan - Friend. A true friend most of all, but there's many other things as well. He's a great athlete, an awesome competitor, and someone that is always there to help you. He has a dynamic personality, and is skilled at everything he does. Lots of things come to mind, everything that Johnny does is memorable and significant.

JWH - How far back do the two of you go?

Stan - I first met Johnny when I moved here to Birmingham in 1973. I sponsored a softball team for several years, and we played softball and ran together. We worked out, trained, raced, and went on trips to races together. And of course all the partying that goes along with that. Like everything else, Johnny could really party.

JWH - You were neighbors for awhile too, weren't you?

Stan - Johnny lived about a block from our restaurant, New York Pizza. He was there quite often. He came up with some great ideas to help me in my business, and regardless of my predicament, Johnny had something positive as a response. He has the ability to empathize and put himself in someone else's shoes. Johnny does this for a lot of people.

I worked with Johnny in real estate for three or four years back in the '80's, but I didn't stick with it. I left that up to Johnny. He has really excelled in real estate, and that business takes a hell of a lot of effort and energy. He's really remarkable.

JWH - Do you still run?

Stan - Yes, but I have become more of a gentleman runner now. I don't compete and I haven't competed in years. I just run a couple of miles a day. I do talk to Johnny about running every now and then. He's always encouraging about my running. At one time we did run together a lot. That was always fun. I think we pushed each other a lot and helped each other.

Johnny has, in the last several years, done more of the distance running, triathlons and such. When he was in college he was more of a sprinter. He was an outstanding hurdler in high school and college, and he was also competitive in the Decathlon. That's pretty remarkable considering his build. He's certainly not built for some of the strength events in the Decathlon, but he tried it anyhow.(laughter) Try, nothing, he did it! He and I are built similarly. We're both fairly thin, like most runners are. I would never have considered the shot-put or javelin, but he was out there doing that sort of stuff. Like I said, he's remarkable.

JWH - Everything everyone tells me about Johnny is so positive. Do you know of anything that Johnny has done that didn't have good results?

Stan - (laughter) One time he and Eddie Elrod were doing their Blues Brothers act at the college. It was one of their very first performances, and I went. It was at half-time at a University of Alabama at Birmingham basketball game. In the first half, UAB scored something like 18 points, they had been terrible, and the crowd was very upset. So here came Johnny and Eddie to do their act, and the crowd took out all their frustrations by booing them. It was even in the newspapers that they were booed. It didn't seem to bother them in the least. Now they perform in front of large audiences, and sell out just about every time they perform.

I also remember a trip to Georgia for a race. Johnny, Bill Gates, and I went to a friend's place, where we arrived at about 1:30 A.M. We had been drinking all the way over there, and when we arrived we fell asleep on the floor. But on the other side of this door were his two rottweilers. They barked all night long, so we ended up getting about two or three hours of sleep before the race. It was a ten mile race on a very hilly course that started early in the morning. We began drinking again right after the race, and spent the day going all around Atlanta and drinking. All we had had to eat that day was a sandwich, so we decided to go to the Polaris at the top of the Hyatt in downtown Atlanta. This was a real fancy place. We still hadn't taken a shower or changed out of our running clothes. We had a couple of cocktails there, but we could tell by people's attitude that we needed to move on. So we started back to Alabama. We were stopped in Bremman, Georgia. Some guy had pulled up next to us with a helicopter in the back of his pickup truck. Gates was impressed by the helicopter, so he got out in the middle of traffic and wanted to talk to this guy. The guy was an off-duty police officer, and he radioed in that we were in no condition to be driving, and were out of control. Bill had leaped onto the trunk of the car, held on to the roof, and hollered, "Go on! Drive!"

We drove just far enough to pull over and get Bill back in the car. We drove another three blocks and got pulled over by the law. I had stopped drinking because I was driving, and I had to do the sobriety test. While I was doing that, Johnny gathered up all the empty cans and bottles-all the evidence-and convinced Bill to throw them away. So Bill started running off with all this stuff, not having any earthly idea where he is or where he's going. A few minutes later he was back at the car. He had fallen on the bag, broken a bottle, and cut his face. Johnny got the bleeding stopped. I then got us out of there, having passed the sobriety test. Then Johnny then tells me we have to take Bill to the hospital to get his face stitched up. In the mean time, Bill had called his mama and told her he was drunk. She lives in Montgomery, and she was terribly upset.

We finally got out of Bremman about 11:00 that night. By this time we were sober and out of beer, and after all that has happened to us we needed a beer bad. But this was a dry county, so we had to go the last town in Georgia that was wet, Tallapoosa. We went into this trailer, that was a bar, and got a couple of beers just to calm our nerves. Of course we drank all the way back to Birmingham, and then went to the Plaza so Johnny could play shuffleboard. He could beat anyone at shuffleboard no matter what shape he was in. That was a trip to remember. Some trips are just a blur, and some I don't remember at all. Drinking and running was a tradition that went back to the Vulture days. That's what I need to tell you about, the Viaduct Vultures.

I think a lot of what we did in those early days was just an excuse to drink. We would go out and run a very difficult and draining interval workout at the track every Tuesday afternoon. It didn't matter if it was 25 degrees or 99 degrees outside, we would go out and run. And we would run to the point of exhaustion. Then we would start drinking. This all happened in the late '70's at Shades Valley High School. We wanted a place to drink where we wouldn't be bothered by anyone, we were bringing coolers and drinking right outside the school, which wasn't such a good idea. Johnny got the idea to go up under the 280 viaduct which ran past the school, so we began climbing up the cement incline and sitting and drinking under the roadway. We would sit up there and drink beer and be separated from the rest of the world. That was the beginning of the Viaduct Vultures, which is still together actually. They don't call themselves that, because their drinking days are behind them. But they still run every Tuesday afternoon.

The group eventually stopped drinking under the overpass,

and moved up to bars. Depending on where we would run, we would go to a nearby watering hole. We got thrown out of some of Birmingham's finest bars. We went to Poor Willy's in Vestavia for awhile. P.T.'s over on Hollywood. Then they started coming to my place, New York Pizza, when I bought it in December of 1986. I think the drinking and partying aspect has pretty well died out. They get together after their workouts, but very few of them drink anymore. Johnny quit drinking, and I think that influenced a lot of the others to give it up, too. Johnny wasn't really our coach back then, but since then it has evolved into

National Guard - 1966

Johnny being the actual coach. It's just a leadership type thing. It was a natural progression because he's a leader, and he's good at it without imposing.

JWH - You must be amazed at the changes in Johnny over these years.

Stan - Yeah. Johnny and I shared some happy times as well as some troubled times. I went through a difficult divorce in the early '90's. Johnny and I both went through a lot of counseling . As a matter of fact, we went to the same counselor. We went through individual and group sessions. I was dissatisfied with a lot of things in my life, and Johnny was going through a difficult time. He was drinking real heavy, and I think those sessions revealed a lot of things to Johnny as far as his feelings were concerned. I think it gave him an awareness of things he had been avoiding his whole life. He had to face himself, and that brought about a major personal transformation.

JWH - What else do you want to say about Johnny?

Stan - He's extremely intelligent and well-organized. He has to be to do all the things he does; real estate, coaching, competing, training, and parenting, as well as being very active in his church. For him to do all of these things at the level he does them is amazing, and I think that has been a big part of his success. He doesn't give himself enough credit, especially for his intelligence.

When I was running this morning I was thinking about Johnny being Forest Gump. The things he does he excels in, and the people he touches remember him. Johnny is one with whomever he is with, and that is a remarkable trait. Everything he does, he does with every ounce in him. That's what he's doing now spiritually, developing that side of himself. That will make him that much more powerful. What can I say? I love Johnny.

Jeff and Sharon Terry
Engineer/Teacher
Lay Pastor

Sharon & Jeff Terry

JWH - Jeff, congratulations on winning the Vulcan Run again. How many times have you won?

Jeff - Four times.

Sharon - No, five times.

JWH - Tell us some of your running accomplishments.

Jeff - I've run in the Boston Marathon six times, and finished as high as 53rd. I was 10th American at the 1999 Boston Marathon. I've run the Portland Marathon three times, and I've finished 3rd there twice. That's a big race with 7,000 people, and I've finished 3rd overall the last two years. I have won a lot of local 5 K's and 10 K's around here.

JWH - Being in the running world, you were bound to run into a guy named Johnny Montgomery. Where did your paths cross?

Jeff - I ran into Johnny the first time about seven years ago when I met him at a race. I started getting into pretty good shape after I ran my first marathon. Somebody told me that I should meet Johnny Montgomery because he can really get you into good shape. This person's name was Wendy, I can't remember her last name.

Sharon - Crane.

Jeff - Oh yeah, Wendy Crane, she took me over and introduced me to Johnny. And she was right because he got me in great shape. I thought I was in good shape, but it was nothing compared to where I am now.

JWH - He must have done you good, because you're winning. Sharon, you're a runner also, aren't you?

Sharon - Yes, I am.

JWH - When did you take up the sport?

Sharon - A year or so after Jeff started. I run marathons as well. I also train with Johnny.

JWH - Has he helped you?

Sharon - Oh absolutely, oh yes.

JWH - Johnny just got back from competing in his 8th Ironman competition. Do either of you have aspirations of competing in the Ironman?

Jeff - Not me

Sharon - No, marathons are about it for us.

Jeff - I don't think either one of us has the time or the determination to do what they do. Training for running is one thing, but when you add two more sports on to it, it takes it to a newer level.

Sharon - There's also a time factor involved. We still have young children.

JWH - Jeff, I know that you are an engineer in the transportation industry. Sharon, where do you work?

Sharon - I teach high school English at Woodlawn High School, and I'm a commissioned lay pastor for the Edgewood Presbyterian Church.

JWH - You are both very busy people.

Jeff - It's hard enough to find the time to train for the marathons. To add two more sports to our schedules would be impossible.

Sharon - Especially with both of us training for marathons. It's very difficult to get in that many miles with three jobs and three children.

JWH - My hat's off to you. You have seen changes come for Johnny, notably in his spiritual life.

Sharon - I'm just so happy for Johnny. I can tell he's a much happier person, because of his priorities, which are in order. I think that has made a difference in all aspects of his life. From his running, to his work, to his personal relationships, they've all been affected. We didn't know Johnny when he was drinking, but I can tell he's made a change even in the last couple of years. I think that he has strengthened his commitment to the church and to the Lord. Even in the last year I've seen changes in Johnny.

JWH - Jeff, what would you like the world to know about Johnny?

Jeff - Johnny is one of the most motivating and inspirational people you could ever meet. He works very hard, not just at his running, swimming, and biking, but also in his job. He's very, very successful in the real estate business. He's well known in this town, I don't think there's anyone in Homewood who doesn't know Johnny. I think that says a lot for Johnny right there, he takes the time to stop and say, 'Hi,' to everyone he sees. You can tell he loves people, it's obvious.

Sharon - He shares his faith with a lot of people. That's one of the special things about Johnny. He's willing to share his faith. We've had conversations about his faith, and mine, in the green bean section at the Piggly Wiggly Grocery Store, on the phone, at the track, and a lot of other places. I think that's one of the most impressive things about Johnny. I remember when we knew Johnny, but we were not as close to him. We became close when he sold our first house for us. He took us out to lunch the day of the closing, and he said a little prayer before lunch in the restaurant. That's a small thing, we didn't know him well then, and that impressed me that he was willing to share his faith in that way.

When he was showing our house, he would call us and say, "Okay, I have someone coming to see the house. Say a prayer, I've already said one." So that was nice to know that even in a business setting his faith was up front.

I feel that Johnny will always be there for us. I feel like I could call Johnny anytime, for anything, and he would be there. There are a lot of people who say that you are their friend, and might go out to dinner with you, or what have you. But there are very few people who would actually be there when you need them. I know without a doubt that no matter what it is, I could call Johnny and he would be there. He's the one that we put on the kid's cards at school to call in case of emergency.

JWH - When you put your kids in his care, you can't trust any more than that.

Sharon - They know that if they are ever lost at a race, look for Johnny. Our son carries Johnny's business card in his wallet. If he's ever lost he will be returned to Johnny Montgomery.

Jeff - All three of our kids really look up to Johnny. It's amazing to have an adult of Johnny's stature who will get down on the kid's level. They can appreciate and have fun with him, too. It's amazing to see him with our children.

Sharon - They have his postcards on their bulletin boards and carry them in their wallets, too. He's a hero to them, as well as someone to look up to and a good friend as well. That's a real gift to have that kind of love for a child.

Jeanette Parrot
Sister
Savings and Loans

Jeanette Parrot

JWH - You were like a second mother to Johnny, if I remember right.

Jeanette - You're right, and I bet Johnny never told you that I gave him a spanking when he was about 20 years old. He was still going to Livingston, and mother had been in the hospital. I had told Johnny that I was going to pick up mother and bring her home, and I wanted him to light the propane heaters so the old house would be warm for mama when we got back. So when we got back there wasn't a door open nowhere, and I had to climb a post by the gas pumps to get on the porch. I went in and lit the heater upstairs, the stove in the kitchen, and the heaters in the store. I didn't tell mama what was going on because she thought that Johnny and Jimmy was the only two people in the world. I left mama in the car with the heater running while the store warmed up, and then went back upstairs and got me a belt, and folded it. Johnny and Jimmy always slept naked. I took the cover and laid it back off him, and took that belt and I came down just as hard as I could, and I got me four or five good licks before he came up out of that bed. I had him good awake, and he started getting his clothes on, so I went down and got mama out of the car. She didn't like me whipping Johnny. Mama never did like it when I jumped on Jimmy or Johnny, either one. But I didn't ease up on Johnny that day; I said, "Get a broom, get a mop, 'cause you ain't goin' to sit down today." That night he told mama, "If she wasn't my sister, I'd kill her."

That's the way it was with Jimmy, too. Jimmy got to do anything he wanted to, but when he did something to upset mama then she would tell me and I would jump on him. They were all scared of me because they knew I'd jump on them.

I remember a lot of times when Johnny was in school, mama wouldn't have any money. Johnny would come by here at night, and he would sit around and drink a few beers, and I would give him 8 or 10 dollars to have some money for school.

JWH - When I interviewed Johnny, he mentioned that his brother-in-law had held a shotgun on him. What was that all about?

Jeanette - That was my ex-husband. One night when he came to the store to get me, since I had moved in there with my children to get away from him, because he had been threatening me so much. That day I was giving my son Walter a bath in the bathtub, and all of a sudden he came up the steps. My mother was sitting there on the couch with Janet, my daughter, who was three years old then. When he got to the top of the steps, mother asked him what he wanted. He said, "I come down here to get Jeanette, because I've decided we're going back together." This was in January. Our divorce had been in October. I stuck my head out of the bathroom door and said, "What do you mean, we're going back together?" He said, "We

are, we're going to raise these kids." I said, "No, we're not. I'm
through with you." He went back downstairs. Johnny was down
in the store and he watched him go out to his truck and get a
shotgun, so he ran to the steps and hollered, "Jeanette, run!
He's got a shotgun!" I ran for the porch, and as I looked back he
was holding the shotgun on Johnny. I jumped off the porch of
that two-story building and got myself across that four-lane highway somehow. He held the gun on Johnny while he searched
for me, looking in every closet, under every bed, hunting me.
He held that gun on Johnny, Mama, Walter, and Janet for about
four hours.

When I jumped off that porch, I really got hurt. Somebody
finally picked me up and we went up the road to Sam and Betty
Moore's house. I was paralyzed from my waist down and both of
my feet broke all to pieces. I still have pins in both of my feet.
They called Daddy and the Sheriff's department, and when they
got there it was a stand-off. It took them a long time to get him
out of there. Mother finally told him that she was having a
heart attack, and he told her to go downstairs and get her some
ammonium. When she got downstairs she went out the front
door and hit all that ice. It had been a hard freeze that, January 27th. That was 33 years ago. Elmer Brewer, the county
Sheriff, went and got my ex-husband's mother and brought her
down there and put her on the police car intercom system.
She started begging him to come out, but he wouldn't. Finally,
Nathan Chism, Elmer Brewer, Red, and Elmore Norris went up
the steps to get him. They were some huge guys, too. They
said they never would have got him carried in if they hadn't
got him between the legs and squeezed him until he went down.
They had taken the gun away. That was a horrible night. Johnny
wasn't but 16 when that happened.

For three years after that I had both of my feet in casts,
and had to be in a wheelchair. I stayed in the hospital until
March. After getting out I had to go back again because I started
hemorrhaging. Jimmy carried me back to Druid City Hospital
in his arms. I had to have seven blood transfusions that time.

JWH - What ever happened to this guy?

Jeanette - He's dead. Three years after all that happened, he
called me up one Saturday evening and said he was going to
come out to my apartment. That's when I lived up here next to
Calvary Baptist Church, and I said, "Come on, I've run, I've left
home, I've wound up in a wheelchair and gone through ten

casts, and I'm not running anymore. Come on." I reached up and got my 38 off the chest of drawers and I backed up. When he got there he said, "Open this goddamn door!" I told him if he wanted in, then come in. He did, he turned around and kicked the door open, and I let him get seven or eight feet into my apartment. I shot him in the left foot and the left arm. I told him not to come any closer or I'd kill him. He made a dive for me, and when he did I hit him one time in the upper breast, and one under the breast, and that one went through his liver. Then I shot him one time under the belt buckle. He fell and I walked over to him, and I knew I had one shot left. I said, "If you move, I'm going to put this next bullet between your eyes." He said, "Think about our daughter." I said, "She's over at your house right now, you need to be thinking about her." I reached around, got the phone, and called Police Captain West and told him I had just shot Red five times. He said, "I'm on my way." Then I called mother and told her I had just shot Red, and she would have to make my bond. Well, when Jimmy and Johnny heard about it, they got so upset they jumped up and grabbed a shotgun, and came up here in Jimmy's car. When they jumped out of their car the police took the shotgun away. They never did get that shotgun back. When I went up to tell them what happened, my girlfriend went with me, and we had to leave my pistol with them. They called Judge Nichols and told him, "Well, Jeanette finally shot him." He asked, "How many times did she shoot him?" They told him five times, and he said, "Give her five bullets, and have her reload that gun and go back home." I went back in a few days to get my gun, and they couldn't find it. So I went over to Judge Nichol's office and told him they couldn't find my pistol. He picked up the phone and called down there and told them, "By twelve o'clock tomorrow I'll better have her pistol. If you don't, there better be a brand new one there for her to pick up." But Johnny and Jimmy never did get their shotgun back. Red died of complications from the gunshots.

JWH - Your parents were alcoholics. How do you feel this affected your life?

Jeanette - I don't know. Just because someone drinks, I don't figure they're alcoholics. Mama and daddy did drink excessively. I guess you could call them alcoholics because they drank day and night. Tonight, when I get home, I might drink a beer or two. I didn't drink anything last night, or the night before, and I don't take anything for the pain in my feet. The only thing I take is a hormone pill. I've only been in the doctor's office twice in the last 16 years. A couple of years ago I made the comment that I was the only alcoholic in the bunch now, and Johnny said, "You're not an alcoholic, you could never be an alcoholic, because you might drink tonight, but in the morning you'll be figuring out how you can make a quarter." I never could figure out why Jimmy had to go through that drying out place. To me, if you're a Montgomery you should have the guts to do what you need to do without any outside help.

I really don't know about Johnny's drinking. I'd go up there, and we would all party and everything, but he never drank anything but beer. The way I think about it is that beer isn't really that bad.

JWH - With your motherly nature, do you still take care of Johnny?

Jeanette - Oh yeah, like when Johnny had his throat operations. The doctor said after the first operation, he knew that Johnny was talking three or four hours out of recovery. He was not supposed to talk for 24 hours. The doctor said after the second operation he didn't want Johnny to talk for 24 hours, and I told him that he didn't have to worry about it. Me and Jimmy brought him home that day, and when Ruth came to pick up Jimmy, I told them to hit the road. I told them that we didn't need them any longer. I put me up a sign on both doors that said, 'No entrance, no friends, no company, no telephone calls, no nothing.' So for 24 hours I had him captured.

JWH - What's your favorite Montgomery saying?

Jeanette - For Jimmy it would be, "You can't make chicken salad out of chicken shit." For Johnny, "Always take care of number 1, and don't step in number 2."

Johnny Montgomery
Second Interview

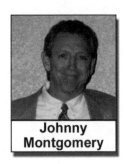

Johnny Montgomery

JWH - Johnny, you've just returned from the 1999 Ironman, which is the seventh one you've attended. While it's fresh on your mind , tell us about it.

Johnny - Seven is a good luck number, and I thought it was going to be one of my best years. As it turned out, it was one of my toughest. There were a lot of trials and tribulations over there this year. I read somewhere that God don't train his troopers by laying them on feather beds. He trains them by making them swim wide rivers, and fast running creeks. He makes them cross long deserts with nap sacks full of sorrows, and if I'm one of Gods Troopers, then I was trained well over there. I felt like quitting a hundred times, but I knew I couldn't quit. I was on a narrow path over there. I had to stay on that narrow path because if I had quit, it would have meant giving up my faith in God and giving up my sobriety. Quitting is not in my vocabulary.

It was a really tough race. I had high expectations, but I didn't do as well as I had expected. But there's always next year, and I'll be ready. When you get knocked down, you don't gain by standing there looking at the place where you got knocked down. You gain when you focus on the next time. Don't keep knocking on a door that's been closed. Don't water dead flowers, because there's nothing to be gained there. I'm back now, a little tired and wore out, and a lot of jet lag, but I'm already searching for the positive aspects of the whole thing. I'm very humble and grateful that I even qualified for this great event, and got to compete with 1500 of the other best athletics in the world. There are 10's of thousands of people that tried to get there, and they had to settle for watching the event on TV November 14th, wishing it was them that could have been there.

Here I am, I've finished 8 times now. So why should I be

sitting around with my lips poked out? Deep down, I'm really tickled with what I've done. I'm a little bit down now because I wanted to do better, but I did the best I could on that day. I know I can do better, God willing, there will be another day. Saturday, October 23rd, 1999, wasn't the end of my life. If it was, I'd be in a cemetery plot by now. (laughter) Anyway, it was good to go over there with my family, and especially my daughter. Words can't express the feeling I had as I turned the corner coming out of the lava fields and there was my daughter. She came running up to me, looking me dead in the eyes and said, "Daddy, I love you."

Of course I cried for two blocks after that. To me that was worth 10 Ironman medals because that was my daughter. Then I turned the next corner and there was my brother and sister. They were so proud of me they had traveled half way around the world to be with me that day. We were bonded together at that race. I've got family, and I've got support, whereas years ago I didn't have any of that. I feel real good about where I'm at right now.

JWH - Did going over early to get acclimated help?

Johnny - I've never gone over there early before. I changed everything I'd done before. I didn't stay at the same hotel that I usually stay at, because I wanted to avoid all the hustle an bustle, and all the hype. I wanted the time to gather my thoughts, meditate, read my Bible, and not get caught up in all that's going on over there. It was a lot more laid back trip for me. That's why I felt like I was more mentally and physically prepared than I had ever been before.

Mentally, I was whole lot tougher going into the water. It normally intimidates me, but this time there was no intimidation at all from the water. And the 112 mile bike ride sure can be intimidating, but there was no part of this race a that intimidated me at all this year. That's why I went in early, to make sure that I didn't fly in on Wednesday and have to be ready to race a couple of days later. It did help, and when I go again next year I'll do the dame thing again.

JWH - Let's talk about the race now. How did the swim go?

Johnny - The swim went excellent. You couldn't have asked for more perfect conditions. In the past, I would have been one of the last in the water, because I felt my swimming wasn't up to par with some of the others. But I had really prepared myself for this race. I wasn't intimidated by nobody. As a matter of fact, in the first 5 minutes I swam out into about 30 or 40 feet of water, where I tread water for another 5 minutes. I had placed myself right behind the pro's; the best swimmers in the world. When we took off, that's where I wanted to be; right behind the best swimmers in the world. I'm not going to be back there with them ol' men and women. I wanted to be up there with the best. I had never done that before, and it took a lot of boldness on my part to do it. I did the swim in an hour and 19 minutes, which was perfect for my plan. It was real easy, "right on" to what I had wanted to do. I didn't have to push it, and I just glided right through it.

About half way through the race I looked down into the real deep water and I saw this fine specimen of a hammerhead shark. I'm talking about a really big one. I said, "Lord, I'm turning this whole thing over to you. I know that you're in charge of that shark, and if you'll just keep him down there, then I'll just stay up here." (laughter) But it really didn't faze me. That's part of my faith. I know that I'm being taken care of, but when my number is called, then I'm ready to go. It may be this afternoon, or it may be 40 years from now, but whenever it is, I'm ready to go because I know where I'm going. I'm just not afraid of dying. That shark didn't bother me, just as the water no longer intimidated me. There were other people that were scared to death, because two and a half miles in that ocean is something you have to respect. I have great respect for that water, but I don't fear it because I have confidence in myself as a swimmer.

JWH - Those pictures you brought back showing hundreds and hundreds of swimmers out there looks like total mass confusion. Is it?

Johnny - Yea, it is. There's 1500 people out there churning up that water. It's like taking light bread to a catfish pond. It looks like a catfish feeding frenzy. It's elbow's punching you, arms slapping you in the face and hitting you over the top of your head. That's why I put my bathing cap over top of my goggles. If they get knocked off , then they'll still be attached to my head. Plus, I carry a backup pair down in my bathing suit. If you lose your goggles out there, it's going to be a long day. Starting with 1500 people is quite an experience.

JWH - How did the transition go from the swim to the bike?

Johnny - When I jumped on that bike, I felt real good. I knew I had to be on that bike about 6 hours, and all I had to do was keep steady. But about 20 miles out, here comes the #1 rated American that had beat me in Boston by a minute and five seconds. I knew that if we had had another mile or two to go in the Boston race I could have beaten him, but, anyway, in Hawaii he came by me at about 20 miles out. He's a better biker than I am, and he was moving extremely well. When he came by me I knew I had to keep this guy in sight if I wanted to beat him and become the #1 American.

That's where I went wrong. I got out of my game plan and picked up the pace a couple of notches. It was faster than I should have been going, and then we hit an extremely strong Trade Wind head on. They blow on that side of the island. About 50 miles later I knew I was dehydrating, even though I was drinking as much Gatorade and water, and eating power gels, bananas, power bars, goo's, anything I could get my hands on, as fast as I could. But I still couldn't get enough in me. I hit the wall at about 90 miles out into the bike segment.

JWH - So wind was a factor?

Johnny - Wind was a big factor. We had one 18 mile pull straight up the side of a volcano to reach Havi, our turn around point. It seemed like it took forever to get there and turn around, but when we did, we had an extremely fast return of 20 miles because the wind was at our back.. But once we flattened out again down in the lava fields we got into another head wind for another 30 miles. It was so tough that what should have been a 6 hour bike ride turned into almost 7 hours. I think it was 6 hours and 59 minutes, and I knew then that I was really in trouble.

At the end of the bike ride. I got off the bike and changed clothes, but I felt wobbly and a little woozy. I gathered up again, ate some power bars, got my running shoes on, filled my hat with ice, and popped it on my head and started running. The first two miles there are the toughest because they go up two huge hills. I ran them both in under 16 minutes, which is a sub 8 minute mile pace, which equals to a 3:30 marathon. That was my goal, to run a 3:30 marathon, because that would be the fastest time in the world in my age group. I still thought I still had a chance of doing a total time of about 11:30, and still make the top 10 in my age group. I kept running, and did real good running through town. My daughter met me at a point in

town, encouraging me, and telling me how much she loved
me, and seeing my brother and sister refreshed me. But then
about 13 miles into the run I started sputtering a little bit. I
knew I was losing it. My legs were getting heavy, and I started
getting nauseous. Everything started coming up out of my stomach. I switched to Coke to see if it would stay down. No luck. I
then tried chicken broth. I tried everything I could think of,
but everything in my body came back up, and at 16 miles I hit
the wall, solid. I couldn't get my legs up, and I knew I was a
goner. There was no more racing in me at that time, so I said

to myself, "OK, let me swallow my pride and ego, and get humble and finish."

I knew I had plenty of time to get in under the 17 hour time limit, but I couldn't even do a fast walk. Sure, I was a little down and depressed because I hadn't done what I wanted to do, so I just slow walked that last 10 miles back into town.

When I got there my daughter joined me and we ran, arm in arm, for that last quarter mile across the finish line. That made the whole thing worth it for me. Me and my daughter going across that finish line together. We've got pictures of it, and we can enjoy that special moment for the rest of our lives. At that moment, with her on my arm, I could have run even if they had taken a chain saw and cut my legs off. I could have run in on the bloody nubs. We made some great memories there that day. My daughter running in with me, and the crowd wildly cheering us on. The crowd was in a frenzy, because they knew she was running in with her daddy, and she didn't care if I finished in 5 hours, or 4 days. It didn't matter to her. She was coming in with her daddy .

Sure I would have like to finished with a faster time than the 14:40 I did it in, but I did the best I could that day. I know I can do better. I have a lot more talent than that, but that was just all I could do that day.

JWH - Let's go back to where you knew you went wrong. Tell me about it.

Johnny - What you learn when you join these 12 Step programs, or any sobriety program, even the Bible, is to stay away from temptation. My temptation came when that guy passed me. All of a sudden I was tempted to abandon my plan, and I didn't resist. At that moment I decided to abandon Johnny Montgomery's game plan, and try to do my competitors game plan. It was just like life. Temptation is around every corner, but when you yield to it, you do what I did. I threw what faith I had in myself out the window. I was chasing the guy, and I was doing his game plan then. That's what I did, and I paid the ultimate price for it. That guy went on to become 4th in the world. He's still the #1 American. When I yielded to that temptation I thought I could beat him. I thought I was the better man and could win. I couldn't and I wasn't. But deep down inside I know I can do better. I'm ready to go again. I'm ready to begin training for next year.

JWH: Johnny, it's time to run that last lap. Would you give us a few words, in summary, that would help others run life's race?

Johnny: When first contacted by you to write a book about me, I was excited about the idea, and humbled. Then I asked you the ultimate question, "Why?" You said that no matter where you went in your travels that if you talked to anyone about running, drinking, or real estate, that they knew me or have heard of me, and always had a Johnny Montgomery story (some of which I am not proud of).

After weeks of interviews you were steam-rolling at full throttle, running all over the place, talking to and recording people all over the state of Alabama, then I became very cooled on the idea, embarrassed, asking again, "Why me?" I'm not that great of a person or athlete, there are many others that are more deserving then I. Then after much praying for guidance and direction, I finally let go of my ego and pride, and thought of the people who have this same disease as I, and maybe, just maybe, this book might help one person in recovering and may save one life, then it would be worth the effort. In I Corinthian 1:31, It says, "Let he who boasts, Boast in the Lord", When I read that, I called you and told you "Let's get going."

This book is not about Johnny Montgomery, but what God has done for me. Yes, I have made many changes in the last few years that I thought I could not do. I never believed I would give up alcohol in my lifetime, I loved the taste and effects of it so much. Who would have thought that it has been over 10 years since my last beer?

The second biggest change in my life is surrendering to my higher power, which I call God. Folks, I'm going to leave with you a few words that help me get to where I am now in life. Surrender – Once I surrendered to my disease, and got out of "Denial" (that means you don't want to know the truth) and surrendered my life to my higher power. It has been amazing the blessings that have come my way. No, your life won't be perfect nor without trials and tribulations, but it will help you deal with them, knowing you are not alone.

In Matthew 6:24, "You can not serve two masters, God and money, you will love one and hate the other." Yes, money is very important, as are material things, but they are not so important that you sacrifice everything for them. It has been said, that I have never heard of a dying man on his deathbed, who wished he had spent more time at the office.

Alcoholism, drug addiction, and suicide, are taking this

country by storm, because this is the easy way out of denial and for those that do not want to face reality. Marriages, divorces, (I call it hitchin', ditchin' and switchin'), are happening at an alarming rate, because it is easier to take our baggage to the next stop, instead of dealing with our problems. If you are living in sin, it is like a forest fire, it will eventually destroy everything in its sight; your marriage, job, friends, and tears families apart, ruins reputation and the children are scarred for life. You can get away with sin for a while, but sooner or later you will find yourself alone, a long way from God. That is why people living in sin will turn to alcohol, drugs, sex, material things, anything to fill that void or hole that is inside of us. You can make a choice and take responsibility for your life, you can do right or you can do wrong. You can live with faith in God or you can live outside God's graces, and live in fear.

I felt all my life I had this huge hole inside of me, like the hole in a doughnut. I felt like I was never good enough, smart enough or fast enough; I always felt out of place. But it was amazing how a few cans of courage would make all that go away. But the next day reality would sink in fast. This disease will make you do and say things you never dreamed of. Now the truth is the only story I have to remember the next day.

Before I became a Christian, I used to question God a lot. How could a loving God give me this disease that I've got? Also too, how can a loving God bring so much death and destruction to my family? But once I became a Christian I understood these things a lot more. As I said before, as Christians, we still have trials and tribulations in our lives. There will be death, heartaches, financial problems, or domestic problems. But each of these, as a Christian, we know happen for a reason. A lot of times we don't have the answers, but in time the answers will come.

My good friend, Sharon Terry, told me once when I was near an emotional bottom that "Blessed are you when your world is turned upside down, then you can see the gospel of Jesus Christ right side up." That was very wise advice.

When these tragedies and heartaches happen, I think it brings us closer to God. Because when you are down and out, God's love is still there for you. Your husband or wife may leave you, your kids may give up on you but God never gives up on you. He will always be there.

Temptation is everywhere. You go to your mail box and you've got five charge card applications at 1.9 % interest rate, or you turn on your computer and its filled with pornography.

Billboards, advertisements of all kinds, tempt us. Temptation is everywhere. Even as Christians, we struggle with this everyday. That's why we must be totally surrendered to our higher power. That's why you have to call on God to give you the strength to overcome these temptations. It's very easy to cross that line. Yielding to temptation puts you on that wide road to hell. The road to heaven is narrow. The road map to get you there is your Bible.

Whenever you are tempted by temptation the easiest way out is just to say no. But saying no before you enter into temptation opens doors. If you stand at that door and dwell on temptation it will lead to sin. As my television pastor, Charles Stanley says, "Sin will take you farther than you want to go. Sin will keep you longer than you want to stay. Sin will cost you more than you want to pay. There is not one single redeeming characteristic of sin. And in it there is nothing but temporal gratification and emptiness."

I've been biking for many years now. They say there's only two kinds of bikers: those who have wrecked and those who are going to wreck. It's the same way in life. There are those that have accepted Jesus Christ and those who have not accepted or rejected Him.

Honesty – If you are struggling with alcohol or drugs then more than likely you have not been honest with your husband or wife, kids, your boss, or whom ever. Because you don't want them to know the real truth about you or what goes on behind closed doors. I challenge you to look in the mirror, look yourself in the eye and ask, "Have I been honest today?" You can't lie to yourself. The truth will set you free. I believe this with all my heart.

As I said before, no matter what I've done, if I tell the truth then that's the only story I have to remember. Because if you are not honest, you're lying, and we all know you have to tell lie after lie to cover up the truth.

If you do have the disease of alcohol or drug addiction, you have to look yourself in the eye and say, "Do I want to do something about my disease or do I want to continue in life the way it is?" You know you're living an empty life. You're leaving a trail of destruction. I challenge you to ask yourself, "Am I honest, is there a higher power, and what can I do about my life?"

The truth is you're losing your family, your job, your house, your car and all your material possessions. You may not lose them next week, next month or even next year. But you will lose them eventually. They are all going to slowly leave you.

That's what alcohol and drugs will do for you.

My last challenge is for you to be honest with yourself. Denial will always keep you a prisoner of your disease. If you need help, reach out to somebody to get the treatment for your disease. The Bible says, "Death will come to you like a thief in the night." Are you ready for that thief? If that thief comes to my house then I'm ready for that race. I've got my race number on; I'm ready to go. Are you ready to go? Are you ready to run that race?

Again, I've lost a lot of things that I couldn't keep, but I have found something I can't lose. I hope and pray that you find the peace I've found. If I can ever help you, please call me at (205) 871-1313. God Bless.

The End

Bob S.
Editor, chief cook and bottle washer

I don't know Johnny Montgomery. Or, I guess I should say
I've never met Johnny Montgomery in the flesh, because I
think I know Johnny quite well.

But before I go into all that, let me tell you who I am. My
name is Bob S, and I live in Tuscaloosa, Alabama. I've been
helping Jerry work on this manuscript for several months now;
doing everything from typing, to editing, to just sitting around
talking about alcohol, it's effects on people, and spiritual mat-
ters that lead people away from that life. I know Johnny, not
because he was born here, but because I've spent many hours
hunkered down in my office chair-the cursor on the 'puter
screen blinking in front of me-as I committed Johnny, and his
friends words, to digital, and my gray cell memory . Johnny is
burned as indelibly in my mind, as a fresh copy of a CD just
popped out of a CD-R.

I, too, belong to a group that, in Johnny's words, ". . . let's
me know that I know there's a greater Power that's going to
care for me." In this group we share stories with each other
about our lives and problems. Especially those problems con-
cerning alcohol. I was told by this group to listen for the simi-
larities between my story and other peoples stories, instead of
listening for differences. We all suffer from the same disease,
I was told, and like any chronic disease, it has a predictable
path it will follow, causing in-common problems for people from
all walks of life and divergent backgrounds. Thus, we all have
more in common than we have differences.

As I got farther into Johnny's story, I started reminiscing
about my own past. I had come from yet another family with an
alcoholic father. Johnny's mother never drank until she divorced Johnny's father. My mother never drank at all; probably
because she never went through with the divorce she so fret-
ted over. You see, my father came within a micro second of
shooting my older sister with a little nickel platted snub nose
.38 special his father had given him for his 16th birthday.
Whatever his reason's, we'll never know, because he couldn't
even remember enough of the scene to talk about it later. You
see, he was in alcoholic blackout from cheap whiskey at the
time.

I also remember him popping caps from that very same gun towards 'the back window of a speeding car that belonged to a guy she had gone out with. All because he was drinking, and didn't like the guy. She had complied to the tee with the guidelines he had set for the date. Even getting back at the ridiculous hour of 10 p.m., which, even my 7 year old mind, knew was cantankerous and mean-spirited. It was the booze making him do it. But he still shot at that guy anyway.

I remember the fist fight he had with my oldest brother over, well, God only knows what that drunken scene was over. I remember all kids of incidences like this, and could go on and on; but I want *because* most of all, I remember hating alcohol so much I would dig up what he thought was his hidden stash of pint bottles, and piss in them. I would then carefully put them back so he would never know they 'd been tampered with. These things left permanent psychic scars on my mental makeup (and probably *his* health and stomach lining) as I'm sure it has for countless others, including Johnny.

And then I became alcoholic myself. Not on purpose, mind you, but because of the insidious nature of the disease. The insanity and denial, the single fold purpose of keeping the drinking life in face of all odds; and *always* laying the blame at someone else's door.

But I digress from my point. My point is, because of my bout with alcohol, I feel as if I have experienced some of Johnny's past as my own. It's one of those 'We went to different schools together,' kind of feelings.

I also feel I share some of Johnny's present; in the respect and deference I give to my Higher Power, that I choose to call God. **He** gives me strength to maintain the faith I so sorely need, not only to stay sober, but to move on and, "pick up my bed and walk," into the unknowable future. I feel peace in knowing **He** is there to help and guide me.

A few years back, I worked for a prestigious educational institution in the medical school division. I worked for them for 17 years, at which time I was summarily laid off. The official reason wasn't my alcohol abuse, but deep down I know that was what it was all about. I can't say I blame them; in fact, they had ever so not casually mentioned my insurance would cover a substance abuse program if in fact I chose to take advantage of it. It seemed everybody *except me* knew I had a drinking disorder. Of course, because of my, and every alcoholics denial, I "didn't have a problem." Everyone else did.

Never mind I was having family, financial, legal-you name

it- problems; and like Johnny, I had a very young daughter that was catching the full psychic brunt of my frustrations and mental insanity. I still wanted to cling to that lifestyle. I was never violently abusive to her, unlike I was to my wife (and vice/versa), but I cringe, and sometimes cry over the real or imagined damage I did to this young soul. She was, after all, my own flesh and blood.

But being laid off turned out to be the least of my problems. My wife and I broke up after I was laid off,-and my unemployment money ran out. So I became homeless. Like Johnny, I was living in my truck, until God really taught me a lesson by allowing the engine to blow up and relieve me of my rolling home. Literally, all I had was the clothes on my back, and what few more I had stashed in a suit case. If it had not been for a friend taking me in; a friend I knew had joined the program about 6 months before, and seemed to be benefiting from it, then I would probably be dead by now. And that's no exaggeration!

When I went into the program, I was told it was a program of paradox's. So, in this spirit-you see, I still thought I knew it all, and everything bad happening to me was somebody else's fault-I desperately tried to grasp what these people were talking about. I was at such a point, I was subscribing to that age old adage, "There is no gravity, the Earth just sucks."

But then for some reason; maybe because the old Buddhist proverb, "When the student is ready, the teacher will come," is true; I remembered an old saying I had heard in childhood, "I'm from Missouri, the show me state. I'll believe it when I see it." So, in the spirit of paradox I was told underlies this program, I changed it around to, "I'm from Alabama, the sober state. I'll see it when I believe it."

And so far it's worked. One day at a time. I now have a small moving business employing a number of people, but I try to use responsible and seriously recovering alcoholics whenever possible. Just so I can pass some of it on. That's the 'giving it away' I do to keep from losing it.

I've by no means reached the heights Johnny has. But, hey, each in his own time, and his own right, if that's God's plan. All I know is, if I trust in my Higher Power, and meet **Him** at least halfway by doing the legwork, He will provide.

God bless you Johnny Montgomery. Your story and spirit is an example and inspiration for me to me. I love you man. And we've never even met.

Go figure.

About The Author

Jerry W. Henry is a Christian, veteran, entrepreneur, musicologist, biographical interviewer, and speaker. His unique and practical approach stems from his personal and business experience.

Born, raised, and educated in Alabama, Henry went into business for himself in Panama City Beach, Florida after his military service in the Air Force (1964-1968). He has also lived in Texas and California where his main focus was on music and music promotions. His collages for music lovers still keep him busy between writing assignments and speaking engagements.

Henry is currently making known the effects alcohol has on today's society. He readily admits these influences destroyed a large part of his life. If only one person can be saved from the strangle hold of this legal drug then his efforts are worth it all, he believes. "We need to confront the alcohol industry in the same manner that we have the tobacco industry," was quoted from a recent speech.

Henry is currently seeking subjects for future books portraying lives that have been rescued from alcohol. To contact him write to:

Jerry W. Henry
4810 Watermelon Road
Northport, Alabama 35473